Inspiring | Educating | Creating | Entertaining

Brimming with creative inspiration, how-to projects, and useful information to enrich your everyday life, Quarto Knows is a favorite destination for those pursuing their interests and passions. Visit our site and dig deeper with our books into your area of interest: Quarto Creates, Quarto Cooks, Quarto Homes, Quarto Lives, Quarto Drives, Quarto Explores, Quarto Gifts, or Quarto Kids.

First published in 2016 by Motorbooks, an imprint of The Quarto Group, 100 Cummings Center, Suite 265-D, Beverly, MA 01915, USA.
T (978) 282-9590 F (978) 283-2742 QuartoKnows.com

Motorbooks titles are also available at discount for retail, wholesale, promotional, and bulk purchase. For details, contact the Special Sales Manager by email at specialsales@quarto.com or by mail at The Quarto Group, Attn: Special Sales Manager, 100 Cummings Center, Suite 265-D, Beverly, MA 01915, USA.

10 9 8 7 6 5

ISBN: 978-0-7603-5179-6

Library of Congress Cataloging-in-Publication Data

Names: Hahn, Pat, 1969- author.
Title: Classic motorcycles : the art of speed / Pat Hahn ; photographs by Tom Loeser.
Description: Minneapolis, Minnesota : Motorbooks, 2016. | Includes index.
Identifiers: LCCN 2016023889 | ISBN 9780760351796 (hardback)
Subjects: LCSH: Antique and classic motorcycles--Pictorial works. | Motorcycling--History. | BISAC: TRANSPORTATION / Motorcycles / Pictorial. | TRANSPORTATION / Motorcycles / History. | TRANSPORTATION / Motorcycles / General.
Classification: LCC TL444.2 .H34 2016 | DDC 629.227/5--dc23
LC record available at https://lccn.loc.gov/2016023889

Acquiring Editor: Darwin Holmstrom
Project Manager: Jordan Wiklund
Art Director: Brad Springer
Cover Design: Simon Larkin
Book Design and Layout: John Sticha

On the endpapers: 1910 FN (front) and 1974 Ducati 750 Sport (rear).
On the front cover: 1955 AJS 7R.
On the back cover: 1957 Maico Typhoon.
On the frontis: 1927 Henderson Four.
On the title page: 1966 Venom Thruxton gauge cluster.

Printed in China

THE ART OF SPEED
CLASSIC MOTORCYCLES

PAT HAHN

PHOTOGRAPHY BY TOM LOESER

CONTENTS

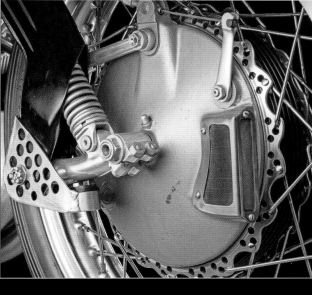

PART I

The Experimental Years

We might think we live in an era of rapidly changing motorcycle technology, but in reality the pace of change today is incremental compared to the early years of motorcycling. While it's an epic sport bike that would trounce the Grand Prix race bikes of old on any track, today's Yamaha YZF R1 has more in common with a thirty-year-old FZR 1000 than it has differences.

In the early days, this was not the case. And that's because the first several decades of motorcycling marked a period of trial and error. There was little orthodoxy in design because no one had yet figured out what did and what did not work. Thus, you had engines produced in every possible size and configuration, from crude De Dion-style single cylinders to complex aircraft-style radial five cylinders, and those engines were utilized in a wild variety of ways, from being mounted in the now-traditional location in the frame cradle to being mounted under the seat, or even, in the case of the above-mentioned radial five-cylinder, in the front wheel.

While most of the innovative designs tried in the early years of motorcycling didn't catch on, usually with good reason (imagine the effect the centripetal force produced by the engine rotating in the front wheel would have on steering!), they did lead to this being the most creative period in motorcycling history, resulting in the production of the most fascinating machines.

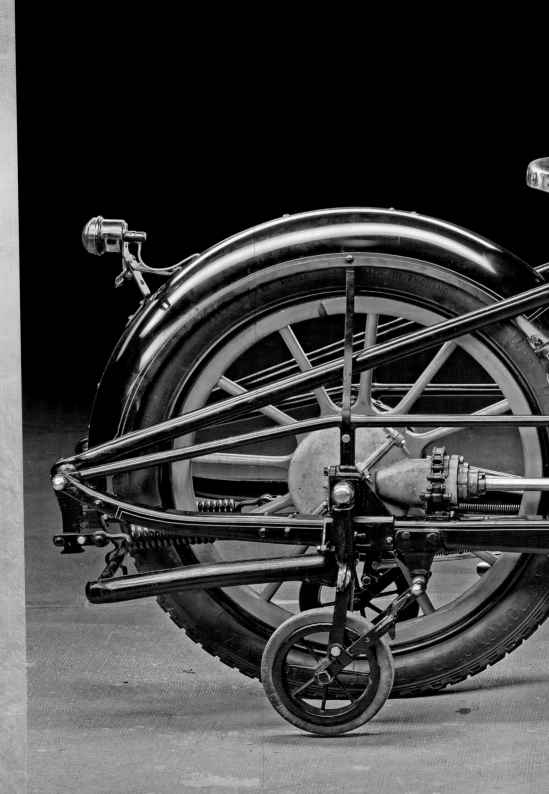

CHAPTER I

1903 Mitchell

I n the 1800s in the United States' Midwest, wagon making was big business; not only was there need to outfit Midwestern farmers, but also to outfit the overlanders heading west on the Oregon and California Trails. One of the biggest builders in the business was the Mitchell Wagon Company. Henry Mitchell was the first wagon manufacturer in Chicago, with a high-quality product that made Mitchell a household name in the late nineteenth century. The company went on to automotive manufacturing, but not before dabbling with the century's greatest invention: the motorcycle.

In 1898, the father and son team of William Turnor Lewis and William Mitchell Lewis (Henry's son and grandson) bought a wheel works shop in Racine, Wisconsin, renamed it, and began making the transition from animal-drawn wagons to human- and gasoline-powered machines. The factory was first used to build bicycles, then quickly moved on to motorized bicycles and, by 1899, motorcycles, though their first motorized machines were actually slower than the fastest bicycles produced at the time.

The Mitchell-Lewis Motor Company released its first motorcycle, the Mitchell Automobike, in 1902.

The frame was heavy, but the little De Dion–type motor in the bike could get it up to 35 miles per hour or more. Local bicycle enthusiasts, now growing bored with all that tiresome pedaling, were elated with the kind of horsepower the engine was putting to the ground. This thing was quite fast for its time.

The Lewis team took the bike on the road, showcasing its technology and reliability, and started producing motorcycles en masse, churning out more than six hundred bikes that year. The bikes were popular, in part due to their ability to win races, competing head to head with another well-established marque, Indian. In 1904 engineers whittled down the frame into a lighter, stronger, loop frame, with a lower center of gravity that gave it a competitive edge on the hills and in the curves. And while the bike was still heavy, it could reach nearly 60 miles per hour.

Despite the innovation, the Lewis family's attention had already turned to the next evolution of mobility: cars. The publicity surrounding the Mitchell motorcycles had tapered off, and rivals Excelsior, Indian, and Harley-Davidson had stepped up their efforts to try to market, build, and sell more motorcycles than anyone in the world.

Before Harley-Davidson appeared on the Midwestern scene, Mitchell motorcycles—a household name in its own right—was competing head-to-head and winning races against the Indians, dominant in their time.

Right: Though the bike was relatively heavy, the little De Dion engine could power the 1903 Mitchell up to 35 miles per hour, which was plenty fast in the day to win races.

Opposite page: The 350cc, four-stroke single Mitchell used a simple and elegant pulley and tensioner setup that moved its power from the engine to the rear wheel.

1903 MITCHELL SPECIFICATIONS:

Engine type:
Air-cooled, inclined single cylinder

Displacement:
Circa 350 cubic centimeters

Horsepower:
3.3

Special feature:
Featured a dedicated motorcycle frame rather than being just a bicycle with a motor.

CHAPTER 2

1910 FN

The Fabrique Nationale de Herstal (FN) company is known for its military weapons and ammunition, but from 1901 until 1967 the company also made motorcycles. FN machines were popular in the years following World War II for dominating trials and motocross competition with their lightweight, agile, small-displacement singles. FN was the first in the world to produce a four-cylinder bike and was well known for its shaft-drive designs.

The genius behind the early FN machines was Paul Kelecom. Kelecom's four was designed to minimize engine vibration, notorious in singles, by balancing the position and firing of the cylinders to cancel each other out. In 1905, FN introduced a shaft-drive, inlet-over exhaust 350cc inline four, which grew over the next five years to a 500cc machine. These bikes were produced for twenty years and loved by European and US riders.

The bigger shaft-driven bikes were terrific runners but expensive, so in the 1920s, after Kelecom had his fun, FN switched to manufacturing smaller, lighter, and cheaper bikes with chain drive. FN produced an impressive range of 250–500cc four strokes, and smaller two-stroke singles and twins that made great competition bikes. The FN reputation and reach was further enhanced with bulkier machines, including a flat twin that was nearly 1,000cc, which were used by the Belgian military during World War II. Later in life, FN had a good run outsourcing and manufacturing scooters. FN continued to produce motorcycles, mostly meant for competition, well into the 1950s, but eventually phased them out in favor of its traditional focus, which came to include aircraft engines. After 1967, FN was out of the business of powered two-wheelers.

The 1910 FN weighed about 165 pounds and could go maybe 40 miles per hour, which was quite breathtaking for the day. This one didn't have a clutch, requiring the rider to stall at stops and pedal furiously to get going again.

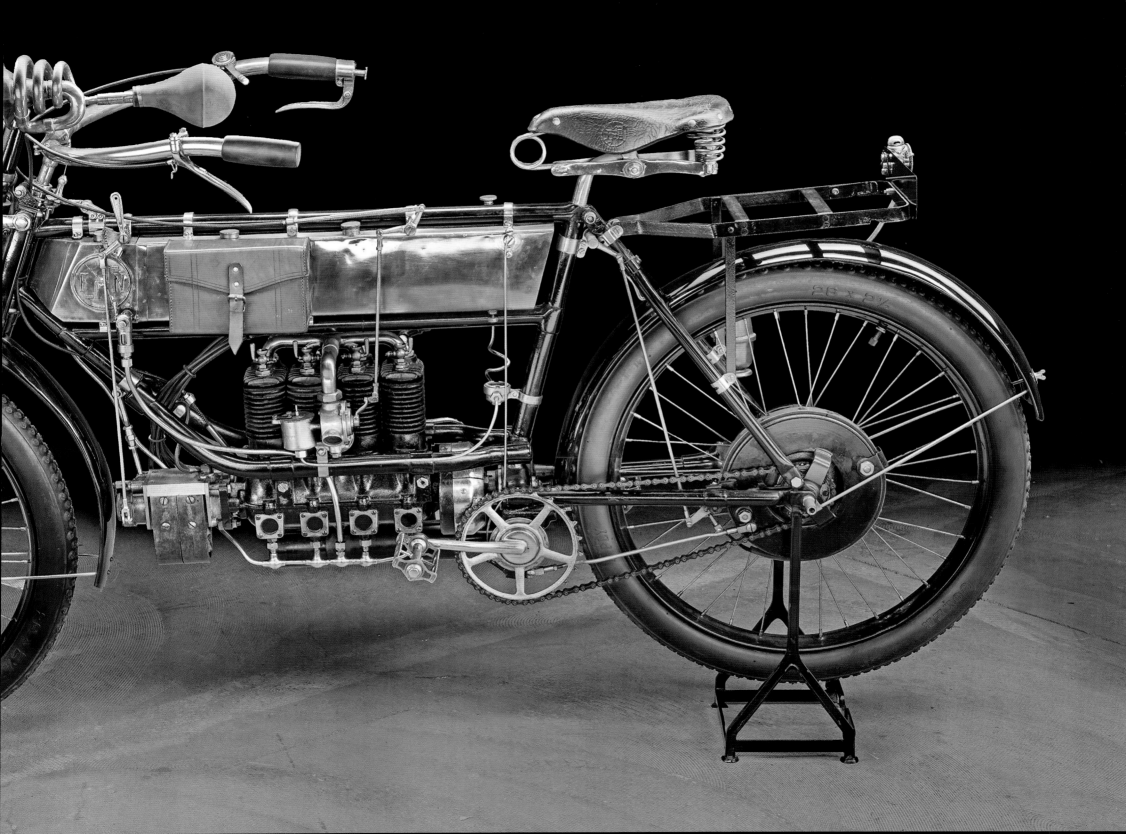

Above: Better known for firearms, weapons, and ammunition, Fabrique Nationale de Herstal (FN) built outstanding trials and motocross machines for more than sixty years.

Right: The FNs were among the first bikes to use magneto ignitions. While originating with inlet-over-exhaust designs, soon FN adopted overhead valves to accommodate higher-revving, faster machines.

1910 FN SPECIFICATIONS:

Engine type:
Air-cooled, in-line 4-cylinder

Displacement:
498 cubic centimeters

Horsepower:
5

Special feature:
FN was first with a 4-cylinder and shaft drive.
Quoted weight was only 165 pounds.

Designed by Paul Kelecom, early FN machines were some of the first consistently smooth-spinning engines. Kelecom balanced the row of single cylinders (and their timing) so that opposing vibrations canceled each other out.

CHAPTER 3

1913 Thor

Just south of Chicago, Illinois, the Aurora Automatic Machinery Company started producing parts and engines for bicycle manufacturers in the 1880s, then began producing the Thor lineup of motorized bicycles and motorcycles. The Aurora company was the sole producer of engines for Indian motorcycles for several years, starting in 1902. The earliest Aurora motorcycle castings served in Indian engineer Oscar Hedstrom's pace vehicles for bicycle races. Aurora even employed Hedstrom for a time, as well as other early pioneers in motorcycle building (Al Crocker, Crocker Motorcycles, and Bill Ottoway, Harley-Davidson).

Aurora Automatic Machinery Company agreed to a noncompete contract in order to remain the sole supplier of Indian engines, so at one point manufactured motorized bicycle kits (for owners to build themselves) under the name Thor Moto Cycle and Bicycle Company in order to remain in Indian's good graces. But when Indian had the production capacity to build its own engines and the Indian supply contract period was over, Aurora launched itself into the early motorcycle foray, introducing the first mass-produced Thor motorcycles in 1908. At first, the bikes used only single-cylinder engines, but the needs of racers and owners quickly led to V-twin engines.

By 1912, Thor motorcycles had evolved into 1,200cc, 50-degree twins with variable throttles, multi-speed gearboxes, and clutches. The early Model 8 was modified through the years to become the Model O, then the Model U. According to legend, a Thor dealer in Utah named Anderson made a daring round trip in the mountains on one of these bikes. Anderson claimed in a newspaper article to have taken the machine from Salt Lake City to Denver on the Midland Trail, and back to Salt Lake City via the Overland Trail. In the early 1910s, this would have been a brutal trip on mostly unimproved roads, through rain, wind, mud, and rocks for several hundred miles.

Thors were able, right off the assembly line, to be tuned for racing, and while the factory never built purpose-built racers, their bikes held sway in Midwestern competition in the years leading up to World War I. Unfortunately for Thor, the motorcycle business became quite competitive by 1908. Before long, the Aurora company—profitable in its own right—decided to quit its own motorcycle business to focus on its other core products: power tools and kitchen and laundry appliances. Production of the Thor ended by 1920.

The Thor Model U first appeared in 1913 with a 1,000cc V-twin engine. A year later, the engine size increased to more than 1,200cc.

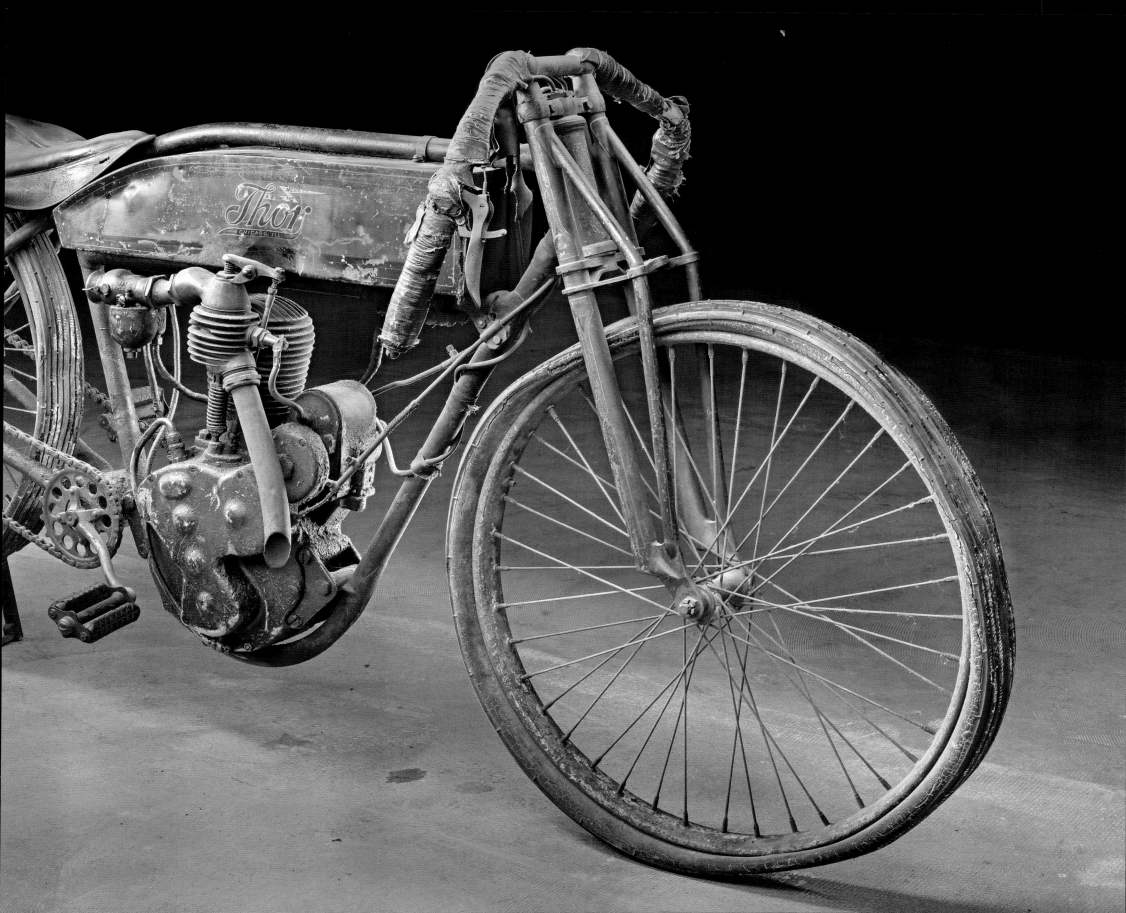

This Thor racer is fitted with an "all or nothing" carburetor, perfect for the board track. You have the choice between wide open throttle and no throttle by either allowing or disallowing spark current to flow to the cylinder.

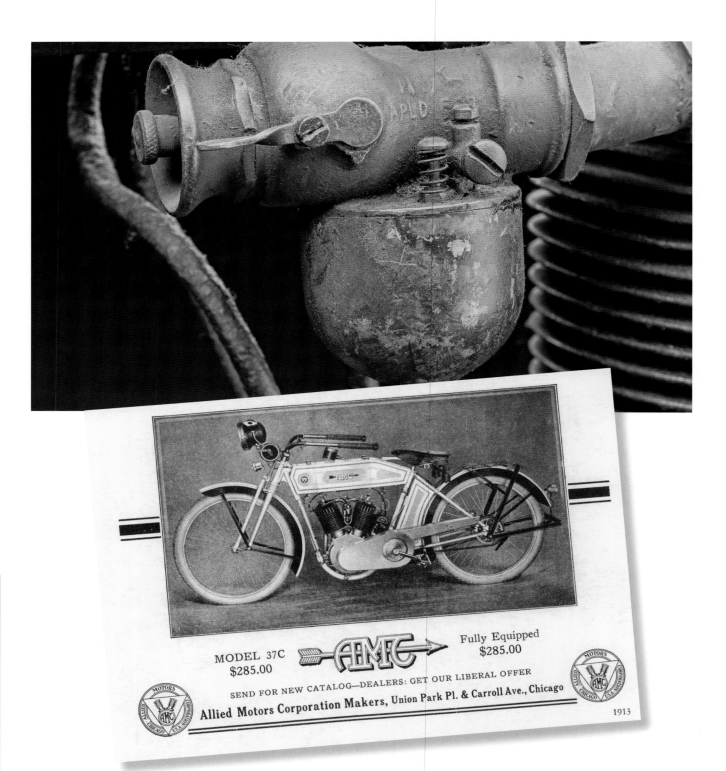

1913 THOR SPECIFICATIONS:

Engine type:
Air-cooled, single cylinder

Displacement:
NA

Horsepower:
NA

Special feature:
Equipped for racing, meaning it is clutchless and can be ridden only at full throttle, or stopped.

New, this 1913 Thor probably cost its owner less than $300 before it was stripped down and prepped for racing.

CHAPTER 4

1914 Indian Hendee Special and 1938 Sport Scout

Oscar Hedstrom and George Hendee joined forces in the early 1900s, and with their considerable creativity and competitive spirit, they began producing some of the most beautiful and iconic motorcycles of the twentieth century.

Indian Motocycles in Springfield, Massachusetts, was the largest manufacturer of motorcycles from the outset of American motorcycle production right up until just after World War I. The first "Indian" machines were motorized bicycles meant to be used as pacers for bicycle races. Hedstrom's designs were sturdy and reliable and sold quickly to consumers.

Early Indian motorcycles were powered by small single-cylinder engines mounted in sturdy bicycle frames. These little shiners were stable and fast, capable of sustained speeds of 25–35 miles per hour with the whole units weighing less than 150 pounds. By 1907, Indian started building bigger and heavier twins, capable of terrific speeds of more than 100 miles per hour when set up for racing. These bikes needed more sophisticated frames and suspension, so the bicycle frame became a thing of the past and proper, tubular steel cradle frames took over, resulting

The 1914 Indian Hendee Special was the most advanced motorcycle ever produced up until that time. Unfortunately, it was also one of Indian Motocycle company's first massive failures. This was the first motorcycle to feature electric start, but the technology was ahead of its time.

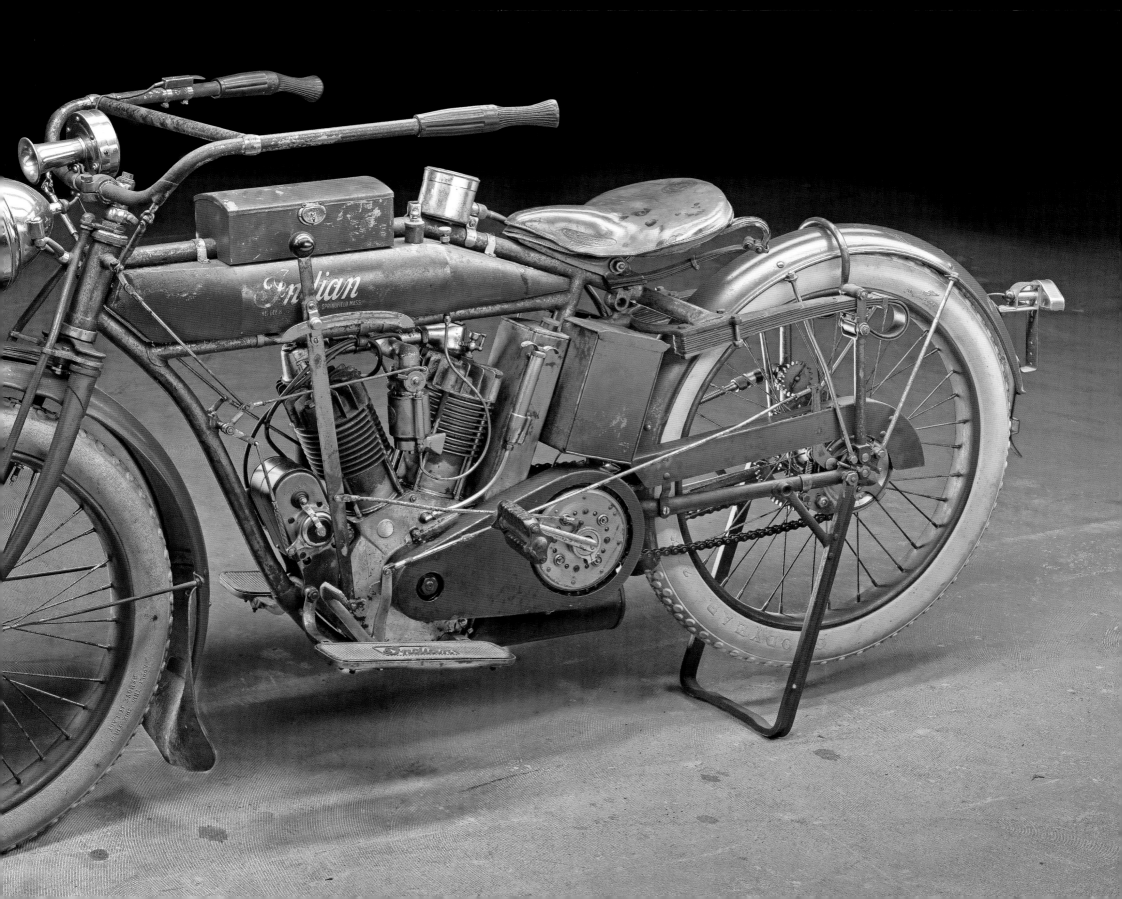

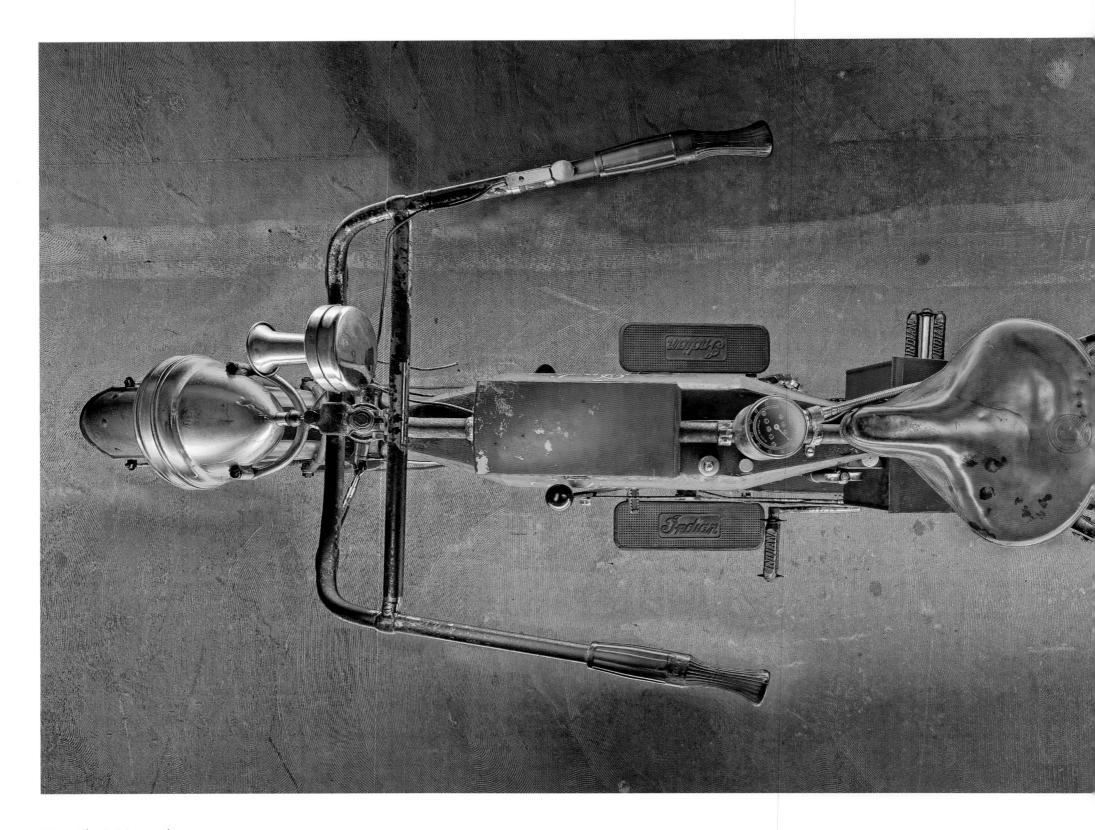

in gross weights of 400–500 pounds or more, with engines displacing up to 80 cubic inches.

Hedstrom also created one of motorcycling's early four-valve cylinder heads, but it was the company's innovative side-valve engines that helped establish the company as a leader in competition machines. Hedstrom was an avid racing fan and attracted talented engineers who shared his enthusiasm, not just from the United States, but from around the world. These included people such as Dublin-born Charles Franklin, the man responsible for Indian's most successful competition motorcycles. Because of Franklin's focus on compact motorcycles with high-output engines, Indian's mid-sized motorcycles made great sporting bikes and were used for board-track racing, dirt-track racing, and roadracing, not to mention hill climbing and stunt riding. In an early demonstration of racing success, three Indians came in first, second (on a machine ridden by Charles Franklin himself, prior to his joining the company), and third in the 1911 Isle of Man. This and other sporting victories spurred production to thirty-two thousand units by 1913, the peak year of Indian production.

It is hard to overstate how dependable the early Indians were for their time—for example, in 1906 an Indian motorcycle was ridden from San Francisco to New York in a month with no mechanical problems.

Above: By 1914 Indian was using a two-speed transmission with a proper clutch.

Left: That large box below the seat housed two six-volt batteries. This was a total-loss electrical system, with no method of charging the batteries; when the batteries went dead, the rider brought them into the house to be recharged. Because the system could only start the motorcycle a dozen or so times before both batteries were drained, it proved impractical.

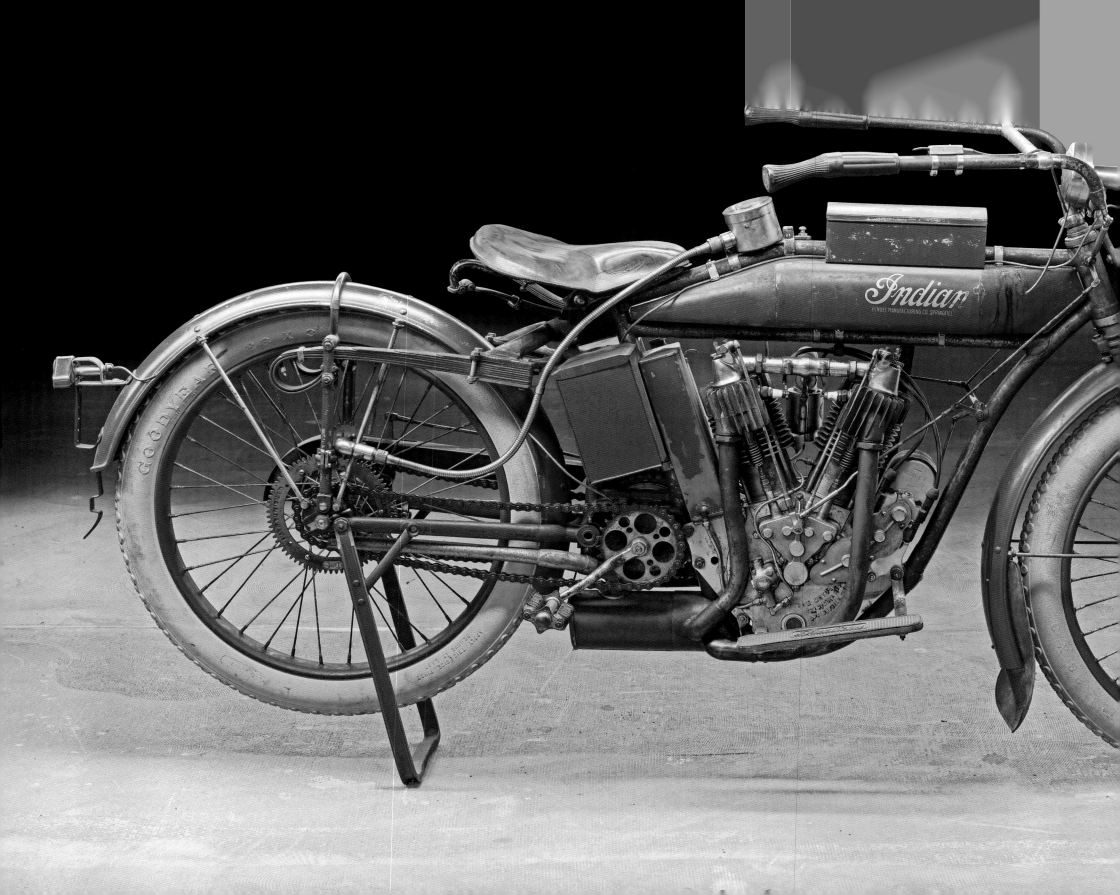

Above: It was Oscar Hedstrom's innovations in regard to motorcycle carburetion that led to the founding of the Indian Motocycle company.

Left: In 1914 Indian was one of the world's largest motorcycle companies, well able to absorb a misstep like the Hendee Special. The company's fortunes would soon take a turn for the worse.

Harley-Davidson was Indian's biggest competitor, but early Indians had a reputation for being more reliable, a strong selling point in the era of cheap Model T Fords.

Indians were durable and well built, able to handle the rough roads of the early twentieth century without breaking apart. The company sold nearly fifty thousand units to the US military during World War I. In its heyday, the company was manufacturing the

1914 INDIAN HENDEE SPECIAL SPECIFICATIONS:

Engine type:
Air-cooled V-twin

Displacement:
61 cubic inches

Horsepower:
7

Special feature:
The first electric-start motorcycle.

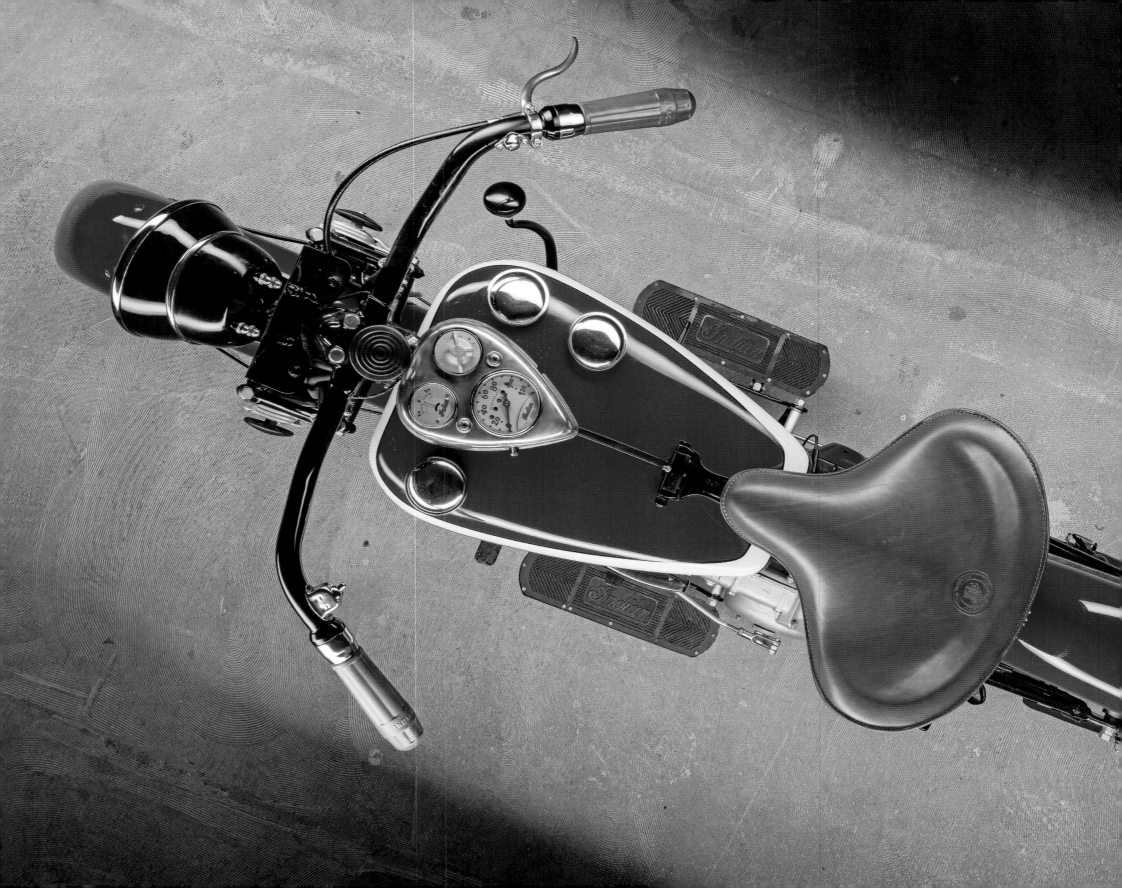

The Indian Sport Scout's 750cc side-valve engine was derived from Indian's larger powerplants, but with a better cylinder and head design and dry-sump oiling.

Left: The Sport Scouts were marketed as lightweight and low-cost sporting bikes capable of everyday riding and endurance, hill climb, dirt track, and road race events.

Standard (Powerplus), Scout, Chief, and Big Chief: a little something for everybody.

The most popular Indian models were the Scouts and the Chiefs, unveiled in the early 1920s. The Scouts were sporty racers—37–46 cubic inches (600–750cc), low-slung, and fast as hell. In fact, in 1967 then-sixty-eight-year-old New Zealander Burt Munro ran a highly modified 1920 Indian Scout up to 184 miles per hour (306 kilometers per hour) at Bonneville, aboard the bike that came to be known

> **1938 INDIAN SPORT SCOUT SPECIFICATIONS:**
>
> **Engine type:**
> Air-cooled V-twin
>
> **Displacement:**
> 45 cubic inches
>
> **Horsepower:**
> 20
>
> **Special feature:**
> The Keystone frame used the engine as a stressed member.

as the "world's fastest Indian." But Scouts were also light and nimble, opening the door to lots of new riders with a relatively easy-to-manage machine. The Chiefs were an altogether different animal— more regal, with lots of chrome. Though competition was fierce, these luxuriously appointed heavyweight twins could never quite compete with the faster and, by then more reliable, Harley-Davidsons after the war.

Indian ceased production of US-built motorcycles in 1953, but for the next twenty years, as various

buyers acquired the name, imported bikes were halfheartedly sold with the Indian name on them. None even remotely resembled the famed bikes of better days. Polaris Industries—famous for snowmobiles, ATVs, and Victory motorcycles— bought the Indian name in 2011 and began building them again. Stylish and true to their original intent, the new Indian bikes have begun a twenty-first century renaissance for the brand.

The Indian Sport Scout was a beefed-up redesign of the "Motoplane." Introduced in 1934, and featured a "Keystone" frame, which used the engine as a stressed member.

Right: The primary drive of the 1938 Indian Sport Scout was by triple chain in an aluminum casing. The fuel tank was also graced with aluminum, a speedometer, and other gauges.

CHAPTER 5
1915 Militaire Deluxe

These unusual bikes were produced, refined, rereleased, refined, and produced many times over by several different companies, or if you prefer, by several disjointed iterations of the same company. The Militaire Autocycle Company started its motorcycle history building bikes in Cleveland, Ohio. While it looked in many ways just like an ordinary—if long, low, and heavy—motorcycle, the Militaire was originally marketed to the public as a "two-wheeled automobile." While the bikes were beautiful and well-built, they never sold well compared to the more practical and aesthetically appealing (at the time) machines predicated on bicycle design.

The Militaire was first introduced in 1910 as the mysterious Deluxe from Cleveland. It sported a pressed-steel frame, hub-center steering, and water cooling, all similar to cars of the era, along with outrigger wheels that could be deployed and retracted by the operator when needed and an honest-to-goodness steering wheel. The first generation of the bike had stability problems due to the weight and off-center location of the engine.

The company redesigned the machine and reintroduced it in 1912, still with the hub steering and outrigger wheels, but with a svelte 500cc single F-head transverse engine. In addition to a curved and comfortable bucket seat for the operator, the rear wheel had one of the earliest suspension systems and used a complex swinging arm and leaf spring design, which made the ride even smoother.

Still, riders preferred other types of bikes available at the time, such as the Clevelands, Excelsiors,

Harleys, and Indians. The Militaire company dissolved and returned in 1914 as Champion Motor Car Company based in St. Louis, Missouri. The next generation of the Deluxe was billed the Champion, with double the cubic centimeters (1,100) and four times the cylinders, with the addition of a three-speed gearbox and shaft drive. Still sporting a steering wheel like a car, this bike didn't sell either.

The whole works was sold to N. R. Sinclair, moved to Buffalo, New York, and the bike redesigned and badged once again as the Militaire. Finally, in 1915, the bike was given a proper set of handlebars and finally looked and felt like the motorcycle it actually was—not a two-wheeled car. The new design was long, low, and sturdy . . . and ran on wooden wheels. Unsurprisingly, this bike never sold well either, so the design was sold yet again in 1917 to the Militor Corporation in New Jersey and aimed at a military career. Unfortunately, the machine was even less adapted to the mud in the European trenches during World War I, and the whole idea soon folded in the wake of the heavy-hitter manufacturers building more conventional motorcycles. The bike passed through the hands of a couple more hopeful manufacturers before finally being put to bed in the early 1920s.

Marketing ad copy for the Militaire described the bike as safe, silent, graceful, strong, dignified, vibrationless, economical, and comfortable compared to "ordinary" motorcycles.

The wooden wheels of the Militaire were a tried-and-true military treatment. The wheels were made from hand-selected, second growth, straight-grain hickory.

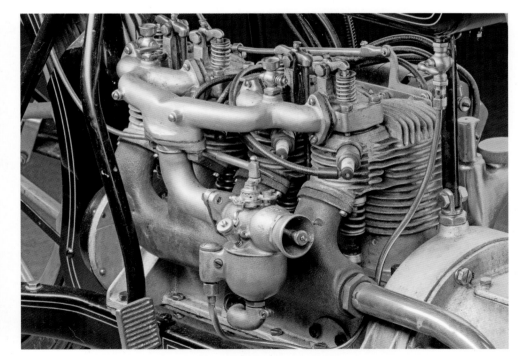

Starting out as the "Deluxe" in 1910, the Militaire designs were built by four different owners in Ohio, Missouri, New York, and New Jersey in seven years, but ultimately lost out to the bigger marques.

A 1,000cc four with 11.5 horsepower, the Militaire featured unit construction, three forward gears, one reverse gear, and pressure-fed lubrication. The intake-over-exhaust design helped with cooling.

The Militaire's idler wheels constituted an attempt to make balancing a motorcycling seem easy and safe. The wheels could be lifted and lowered by the operator while seated.

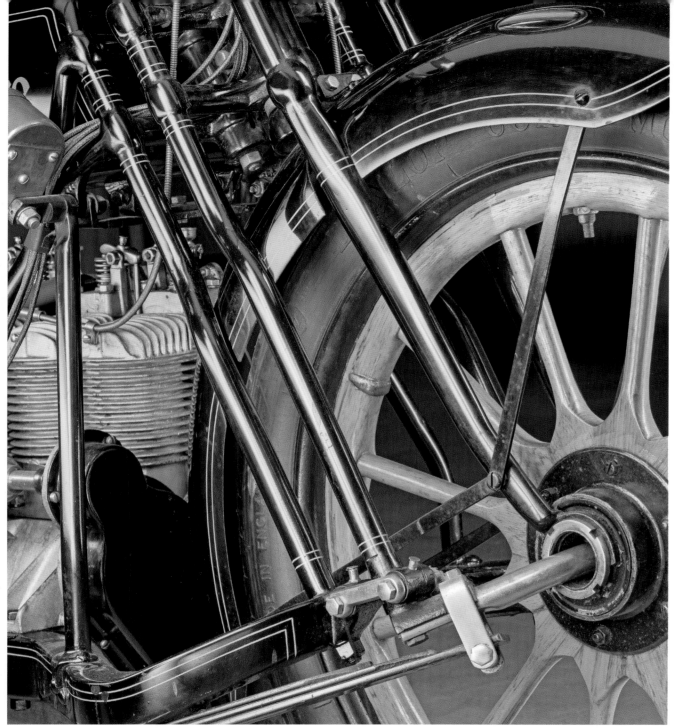

Above: The Militaire designers used a patented, pivoting front axle that made it possible to use a channel-steel chassis, unit-construction engine, and shaft drive.

Left: The heavy steel frame and well-distributed weight of engine, transmission, and drivetrain components gave the 1915 Militaire great balance and a low center of gravity.

The fully functioning speedometer and careful attention to fit and finish set the Militaire apart. Unfortunately, it was just a little too expensive and too much like a car; it never sold well in the US.

1915 MILITAIRE SPECIFICATIONS:

Engine type:
Air-cooled, in-line 4-cylinder

Displacement:
1,100 cubic centimeters

Horsepower:
11.5

Special feature:
Shaft drive, hickory wood rims with a pair of outrigger rear wheels.

Right: Originally billed as a "two-wheeled car," early iterations of these big, heavy Militaire machines sported steering wheels instead of handlebars. This 1915 model was the first with handlebars.

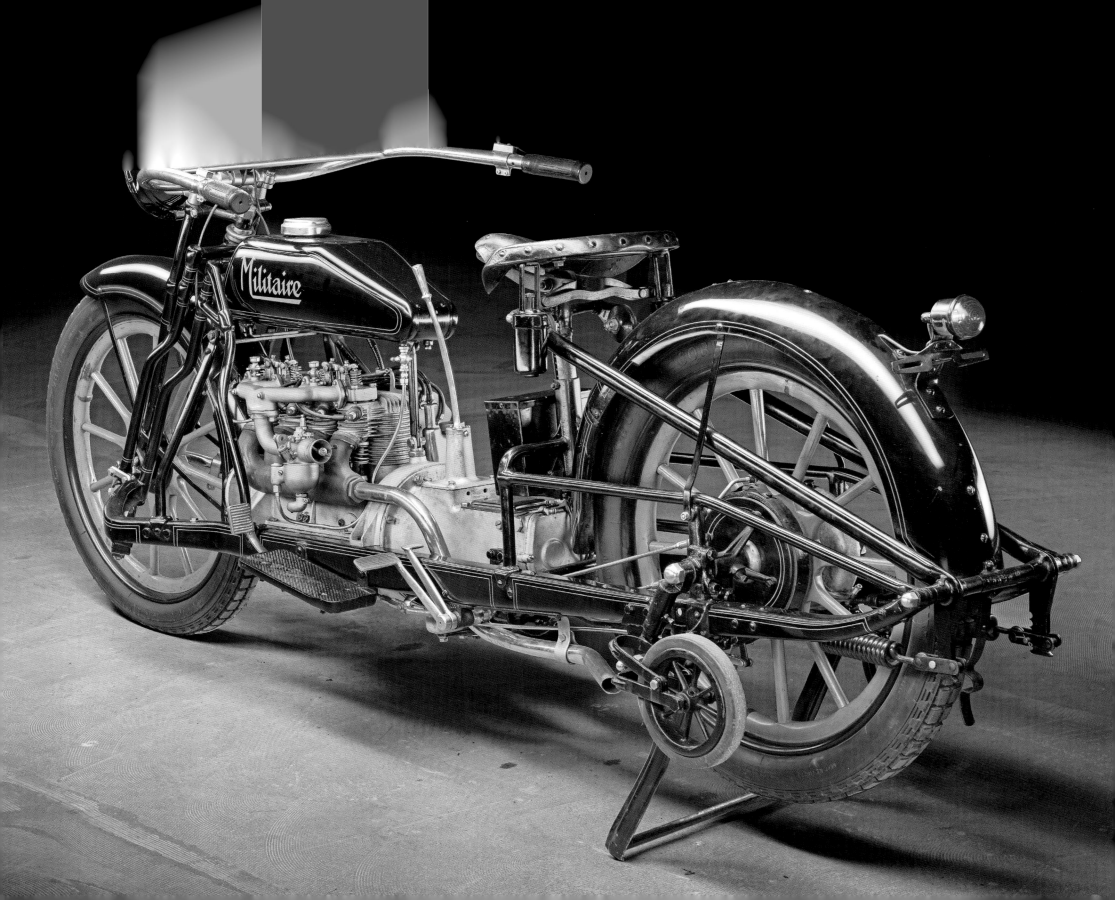

CHAPTER 6

1921 Mars 1000 Replica

The Mars company started in 1873 as a manufacturer of cast-iron stoves, machinery, and bicycles in Nuremburg, and it was one of the first and longest lived of the early German motorcycle makers. Founded by Paul Reissmann, the company began producing motorcycles in 1903, continuing to do so in fits and starts over the next fifty-five years. One of the most striking lines of motorcycles from Europe between the World Wars was the series known as the "Weiss" (White) Mars bikes. The bikes were also available in red and green, but none had the visual impact of the white versions. Starting in 1920, these lavishly appointed Mars machines used a box-section structure that served as a chassis connecting the wheels, transmission, and final drive, with a subframe to hold the engine.

Because of the heavy frame and drive gear, the engine needed to be bigger than most of its contemporaries at the time, so Mars used a 1,000cc, air-cooled boxer-twin engine, positioned in line with the frame rather than perpendicular to it. Only about one thousand of the White Mars bikes were made over their twelve-year production runs. The engines used in the White Mars bikes were designed and built by Maybach, the legendary German car manufacturer. These bikes were technologically advanced, finely appointed, and fast, and the bikes fared well on the national racing scene.

After Germany went through its trying economic bout of hyperinflation in the 1920s, the company's management changed hands and motorcycle production continued, albeit with smaller bikes in the 200, 500, and 600cc ranges, which were more useful and affordable during the years between the wars. After World War II, Mars continued to manufacture their own bikes using brought-in engines and did a brisk trade of small 50–200cc bikes, perfect for postwar consumption and transportation needs.

When Mars quit motorcycle production in 1958, the last of its products, the tiny Monza 50, lived on for several years under the Gritzner brand.

The Mars bikes were among the few two-wheelers to carry a spare. There was even a glove compartment for the safe passage of the operator's personal items.

The box-section steel frame also held the fuel and oil reservoirs. The transmission had two clutches, two chains, and two gears for high or low speed.

As lavish during the day as the high-end Brough Superiors, the Mars A20 used a trailing link fork and no rear suspension and was started by the operator turning a hand crank.

1921 MARS 1000 REPLICA SPECIFICATIONS:

Engine type:
Air-cooled, in-line boxer-twin cylinder

Displacement:
986 cubic centimeters

Horsepower:
NA

Special feature:
A glove compartment and a spare wheel and tire strapped to the rear rack.

CHAPTER 7

1922 Megola

The Megola motorcycle is a concept bike that should have been a one-off, but was actually produced in great numbers (two thousand!) from 1921 to 1925 in Munich, Germany. The name derives from the last names of its three designers: Hans Meixner (Me), Friedrich "Fritz" Gockerell (Go), and Otto Landgraf (La). In all the world of motorcycling, there has never been any other serious effort to mount a rotary engine directly to the front wheel. In one fell swoop, the engineers solved the cooling problem that bedeviled many other multi-cylinder bikes. The Megola team thought it had seen the future of motorcycles in this design.

The inventors had originally designed a three-cylinder engine mounted to the rear wheel, but the idea evolved into five cylinders on the front wheel by the time production began. The four-stroke, 650cc engine evokes early aircraft engines, with a rotary configuration of five cylinders that rotate along with the front wheel around a bearing assembly. The engineers did away with the clutch, so the bike needed to be push started or its wheel spun in the air to start, and in order to stop the engine, the operator needed to slow the bike to a stall. The engineers also did away with the concept of a transmission, linking the crankshaft to the front axle at a one-sixth ratio for top speeds of 50–80 miles per hour, depending on the year of the bike.

This rotation turned the crankshaft, which served as the axle, and the wheel. The wheel spokes are actually mounted on the engine case. A hand-controlled throttle mechanism worked with the hollow crankshaft as an air intake for the cylinders. While it may seem a bizarre and complex design when other simpler configurations would work better, the bike was also rather competitive, like the Mars, not on an international scale, but the Megola won races at home in Germany. Because the bike had no transmission, when racers needed a different gearing ratio, they used different-sized rims to add or remove speed or torque.

To minimize the difficulties of fixing a front-wheel flat tire without removing the engine, the Megola also used a unique tube design that was not continuous; it began and ended without completing a circle, much like a Kielbasa sausage. The pressed-steel frame held the fuel, which was fed to an auxiliary tank and then a priming mechanism, which was pumped by hand. Bumps to front suspension were softened by semielliptical springs, and the engine assembly was mounted on a type of leaf spring. Touring models had sprung rear wheels, while the sport model had no rear suspension and a more powerful engine. With little room at the front wheel for any kind of braking mechanism, two independent brakes were located on the rear wheel. Standard equipment also included an ammeter, fuel gauge, and tachometer

The Megola motorcycles had only a four-year run, cut short by Germany's economic woes in the early 1920s and the factory having to close. Later, smaller two-stroke singles with a more conventional design were introduced under the Cockerell (Gockerell) name, but none of the designs were commercially as viable as successful German brands such as BMW, and the company never gained the momentum it needed for a longer run at motorcycle history.

Previous page: The 1922 Megola was a work of art that also served as a fully functioning and mass-produced motorcycle. Three clever designers combined efforts to create this one-of-a-kind machine.

Below: Touring Megolas had sprung front and rear wheels, a bucket saddle, and long floorboards for comfort. The fit and finish were top notch; the gauges were standard equipment.

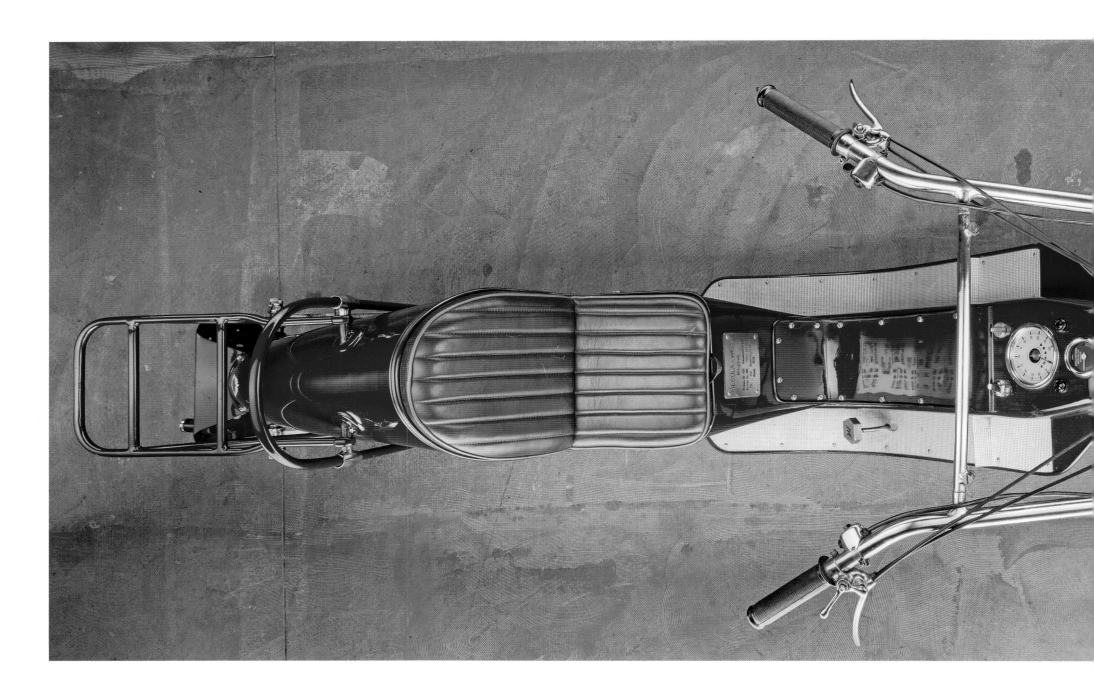

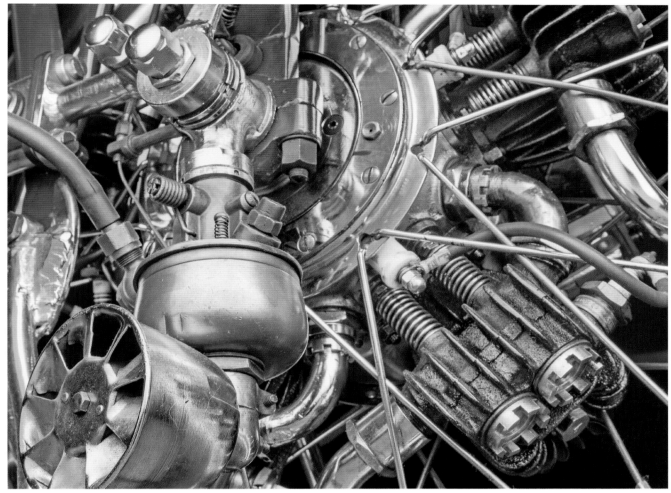

Above: All the engine and drive gear of the Megolas were centered on the front wheel. Without a clutch, the front wheel needed to be spun to get started, and every full stop required an engine stall.

1922 MEGOLA SPECIFICATIONS:

Engine type:
Air-cooled, rotary 5-cylinder

Displacement:
640 cubic centimeters

Horsepower:
14

Special feature:
Inventive 5-cylinder engine in the front wheel; no clutch or gearbox.

CHAPTER 8

1922 Motosacoche

Motosacoche, founded in 1899 in Geneva by brothers Henri and Armand Dufaux, who went on to build helicopters and airplanes, first found commercial success in the form of a self-contained engine and housing meant to be fitted to an ordinary bicycle. Legend has it that the little four-stroke single and its accoutrements looked a bit like somebody's lunch in a sack, leading to the name Motosacoche ("engine in a bag"). The company became well-known as a supplier of ready-made engines for other motorcycles, specifically the Motosacoche Acacias Genève (MAG), which powered early European bikes of other makes such as Ariel, Brough, Enfield, Matchless, Neander, and Triumph.

By the 1920s, the company was producing its own motorcycles. When the very first Bol d'Or endurance race was held in Paris, the surprise winner was on a 500cc Motosacoche, which won the race after running for more than 750 miles. By 1928 Motosacoche had won two European Grand Prix titles in 350 and 500cc classes. While there were at least a couple of factory racing bikes, the company focused on building everyday, practical, and reliable road-going motorcycles. The company went on to boast an all-told lineup of more than forty models over twenty years, mostly inlet-over-exhaust and overhead valve singles and twins ranging from 200 to 850cc.

The company was not able to successfully conceive and sell motorcycles in the lean years of the 1930s. Efforts to improve and upgrade the motorcycles to compete in the European market were somewhat halfhearted. While the company went on to produce thousands of MAG engines for various other manufacturers, its efforts effectively ended before World War II and never regained traction.

While much of the fine trim of this 1922 Motosacoche appears to be weathered brass, it's actually steel, stained gold from cigarette smoke due to sitting on display in a tavern for twenty years.

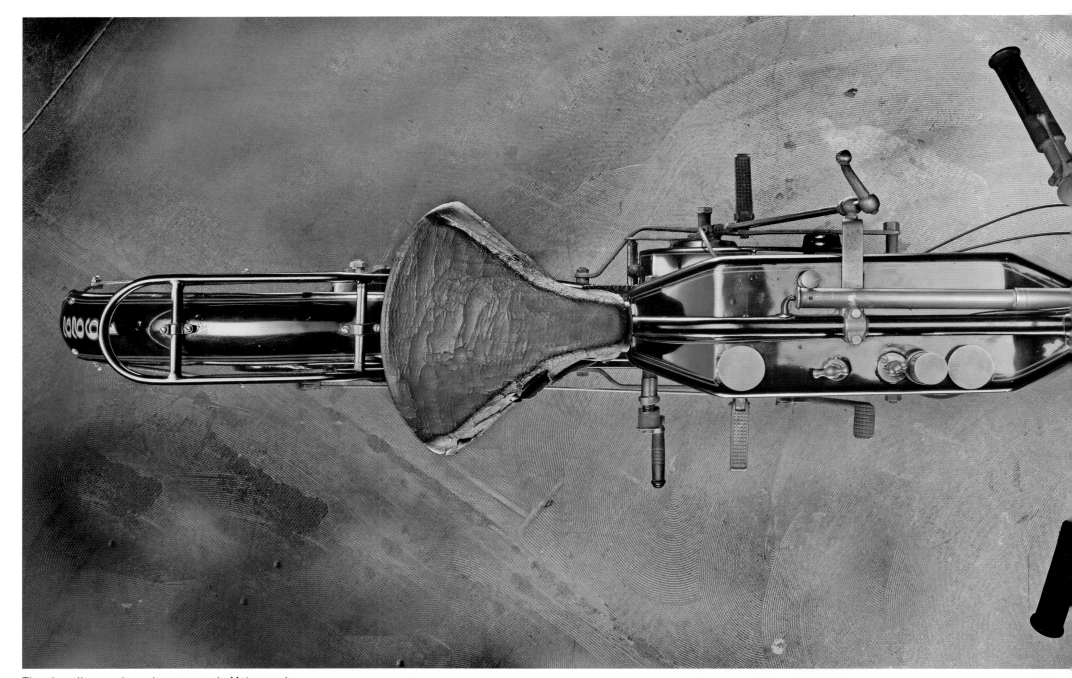

The clean lines and running gear made Motosacoche
motorcycles the most popular bikes in Switzerland. The
company, ultimately, became much better known in Europe
from its export of MAG engines.

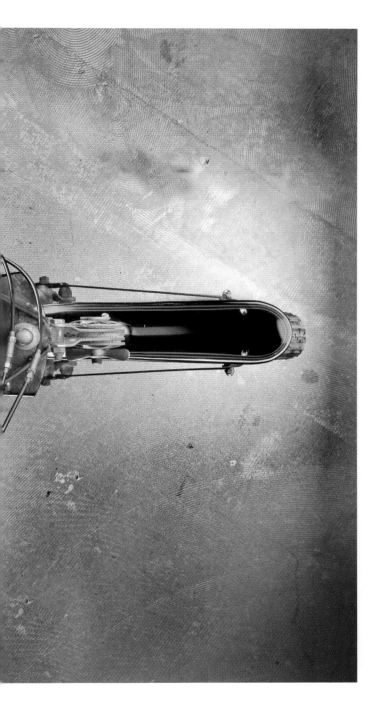

This Motosacoche was restored in the 1980s by Kenny Howard, better known as "Von Dutch," the legendary motorcycle mechanic, restorer, fabricator, and custom painter

Like many of its competitors at the time, this 500cc V-twin, Motosacoche 2C7 used a hand crank to turn the starter. Power went to the wheel via a three-speed gearbox and clutch.

1922 MOTOSACOCHE SPECIFICATIONS:

Engine type:
Air-cooled V-twin

Displacement:
496 cubic centimeters

Horsepower:
NA

Special feature:
Custom paint by Kenny Howard, better known as "Von Dutch."

CHAPTER 9

1923 James

In 1880, Harry James founded the James Cycle Company in Birmingham, England, intending to build penny-farthing bicycles. The company quickly became profitable and went on to produce a variety of everyday safety bicycles and lightweight racing bicycles. By the turn of the century, gasoline-powered engines had become more readily available from companies such as Minerva, Derby, and FN, and the James Company began a long run of motorcycle production.

While the James Cycle Company produced primarily smaller bikes with two-stroke engines from 100–250cc, the company did explore the big-bore possibilities of four-stroke 500–600cc singles and twins, some with cylinders that earned the nickname "pineapples" for their cooling-fin design. These models were advertised as "single-track automobiles," with center-hub steering, sprung front suspension, and front and rear brakes, the best known of which were the Tourist and the TT, also known for their signature maroon finish.

During World War I, James produced motorcycles for the Belgian and Russian armed forces, as well as pedal cycles for Allied militaries. James also still churned out a copious number of bicycles, tricycles, tandem bikes, and delivery bikes. After the war, the company produced many small singles and larger twins without ever really taking hold of the European market, though its 100cc autocycle, really a motorized bicycle, was a hit. During World War II, the factory supported the Allied effort by producing armaments and aircraft parts while continuing to

build motorcycles. Some of these bikes, in particular the lightweight 125cc Clockwork Mouse, served during wartime, and a great number of 100cc autocycles were deployed for civilian work.

After the war, James gave up on the idea of four strokes and focused almost exclusively on two-stroke designs to satisfy the masses. The old prewar 100cc autocycle design was rereleased in Standard and Superlux versions, with a low price and powerful Villiers engine of the type that was in high demand in the late 1940s and early 1950s. When James suffered financial troubles, the Associated Motorcycle Company (AMC) took over the company, which helped it along for a few more years with a steady supply of engines for its small-displacement postwar models, such as the Comet, Commodore, Cadet, Captain, Colonel, Cotswold, and Commando. The girder forks that adorned the James line were abandoned by 1950 in favor of telescopic forks, which used rubber bushings rather than springs, for suspension duty.

Like many of the lesser-known and less-powerful English motorcycle makes of the twentieth century, James was never in a position to survive the postwar onslaught of domestic and imported motorcycles. When AMC went bankrupt, the James marque disappeared for good.

After World War I, James production focused on two engines, one the traditional 500cc version and the other a 650. Both ran gearboxes with three forward-speed all-chain drives.

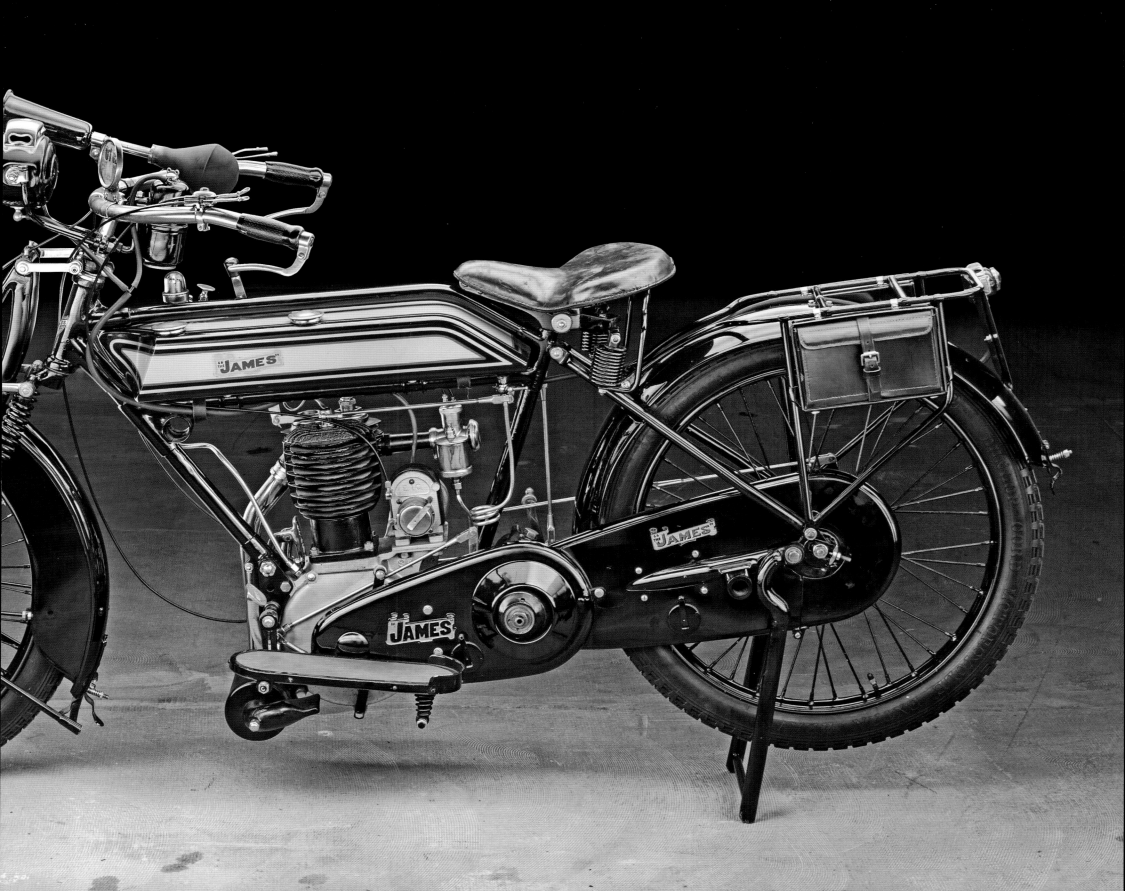

Elegant details abound on a James motorcycle.

Above: Most of James's engines were produced by other manufacturers such as Minerva, FN, Villiers, and AMC. The distinctive fin design on the cylinders earned them the nickname "pineapples."

Left: The James Company built motorcycles for more than sixty years before being dragged down into the financial abyss by AMC in 1966.

1923 JAMES SPECIFICATIONS:

Engine type:
Air-cooled, vertical single cylinder

Displacement:
558 cubic centimeters

Horsepower:
NA

Special feature:
Unique engine cylinder finning earned this James the nickname "Pineapple."

CHAPTER 10

1924 Moto Guzzi C4V 500cc, 1947 Bicylindrica, 1955 V-8 Replica, and 1956 250 DOHC

Throughout the early years of motorcycling, Italian bikes dominated racing and set the bar for performance and style, but were not able to capitalize on their racing success and bring that performance and style to the rest of the world until much later. With, however, one notable exception: Moto Guzzi.

Moto Guzzi motorcycles were the dream of three Italian friends serving together in World War I. Carlo Guzzi, Giorgio Parodi, and Giovanni Ravelli planned to finance, build, market, and mass produce a new type of machine meant to win races. The partners incorporated Moto Guzzi in 1921, in Genoa, Italy. Although Ravelli died unexpectedly in the first days after World War I, Guzzi and Parodi went on to great success, using the eagle's wings of the Italian air force in the company emblem to honor their fallen partner.

Throughout its earlier production years, the company always paid significant attention to building and providing race bikes to both the

factory team and privateers. The first half of the company's timeline, from 1921 until the mid-1960s, was dominated by production of simple, horizontal, 250–500cc singles. Moto Guzzi built more elaborate machines in very small numbers for racing, including an astonishing V-8 prototype, but there was little need: Guzzi's early singles were devastating to the competition due to their light weight and agility at high speeds.

Racing was a passion for Moto Guzzi. Overall, riders on their machines won a total of more than three thousand races worldwide, including fourteen world championships and eleven Isle of Man TT events. Other Italian marques such as Benelli, Gilera,

The early Moto Guzzi four-valves were dominant in roadracing, endurance racing, and hillclimbing. The legendary 500cc singles churned out more than 20 horsepower for speeds upwards of 90 miles an hour.

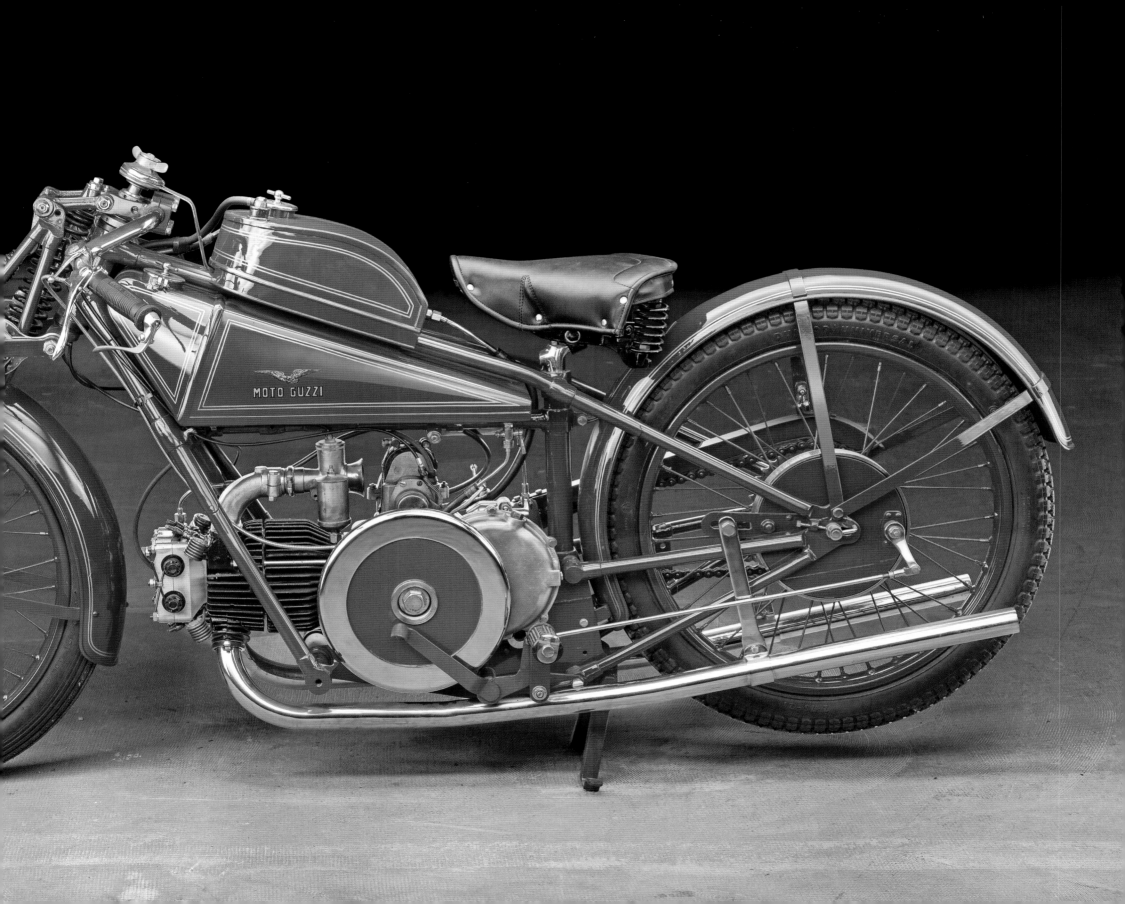

Mondial, and MV Agusta won no small share of races too. On the public roadways, it was the bright red Guzzi Falcone, with a smooth and consistent power delivery, that ordinary riders loved.

Motorcycle racing and production in Italy was dormant in the early 1940s, while World War II and an Italian civil war ran their course. In Europe's lean years after the war, efficient, inexpensive motorcycles were in high demand. Moto Guzzi continued to produce small bikes.

A key to Moto Guzzi's success was Umberto Todero, one of most prolific and respected designers of his time. Todero worked more than sixty years for the company, originally as a factory race mechanic in the 1950s, then lending his talents to the design of new motorcycles, from the legendary 500cc V-8 racer to the iconic transverse twins that came to define Moto Guzzi.

The V-8 in particular proved a high-water mark in motorcycle engineering. In an age when most race bikes were singles churning out maybe 50 horsepower, the V-8 put down nearly 80 horsepower, revving to more than 12,500 rpm and timed at 175 miles per hour in 1957. The project never saw a podium win, due to Guzzi and other Italian manufacturers dropping out of racing in 1957.

Right: Beautiful and functional, the frame's downtubes were spread wide and braced to support the engine, giving the 1924 Moto Guzzi four-valve racer a particularly strong chassis for its day.

Below: The Guzzi's engine, a horizontal 500cc, four-stroke single, had a four-valve cylinder head. The engine was known for being sturdy and strong but required careful tuning.

1924 MOTO GUZZI C4V 500CC SPECIFICATIONS:

Engine type:
Air-cooled, forward-facing horizontal single cylinder

Displacement:
500 cubic centimeters

Horsepower:
20-plus

Special feature:
External flywheel on the left side.

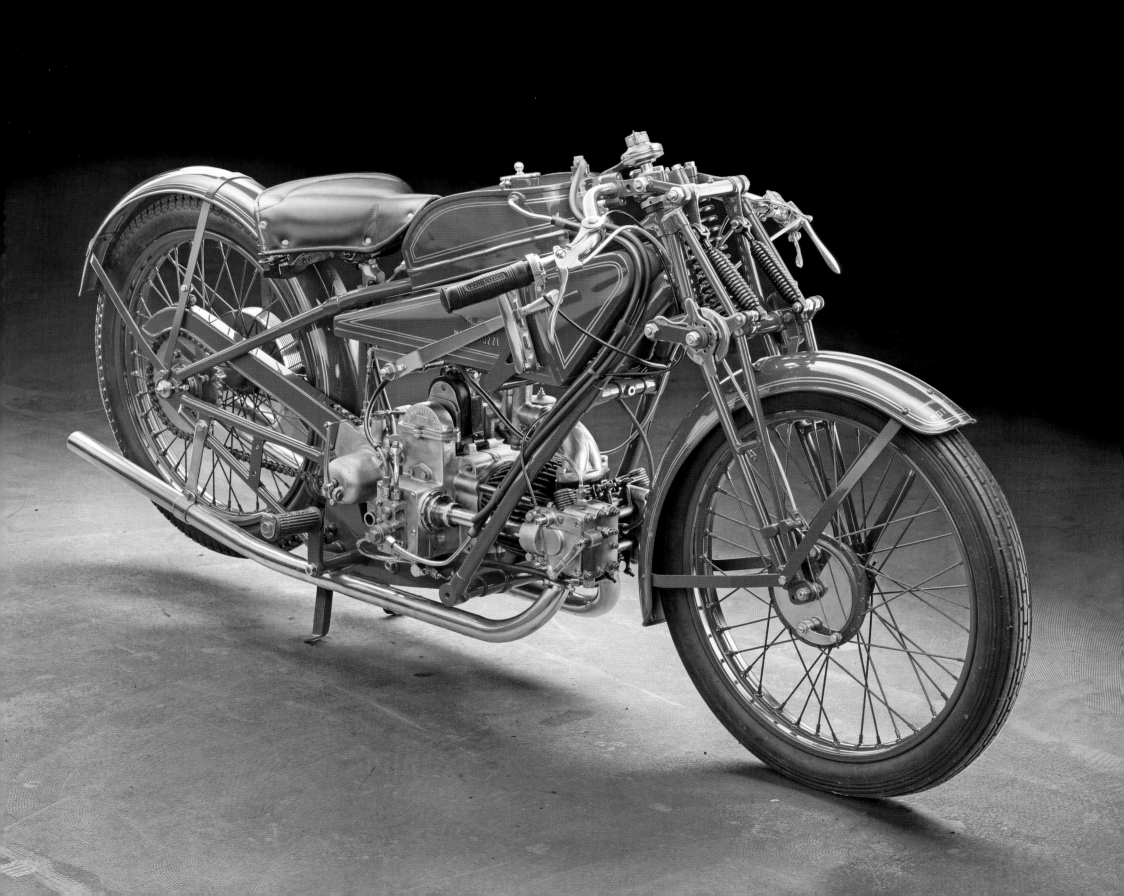

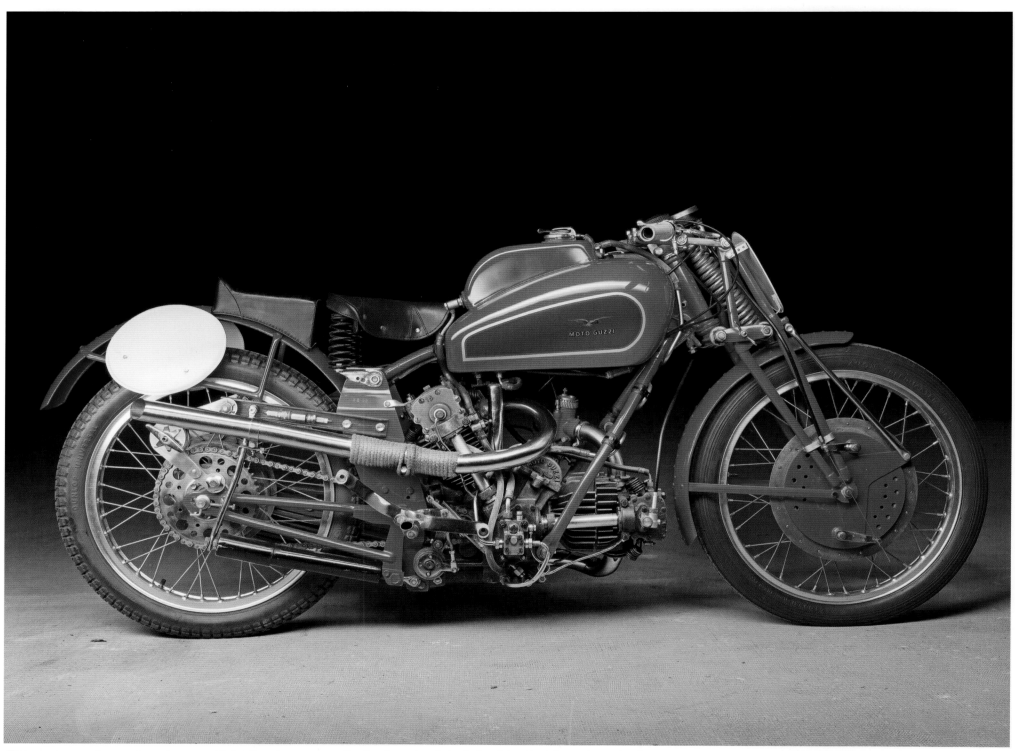

The rear suspension used a swingarm with friction dampers and the front used a girder fork, giving the bike a short wheelbase that made for excellent maneuverability.

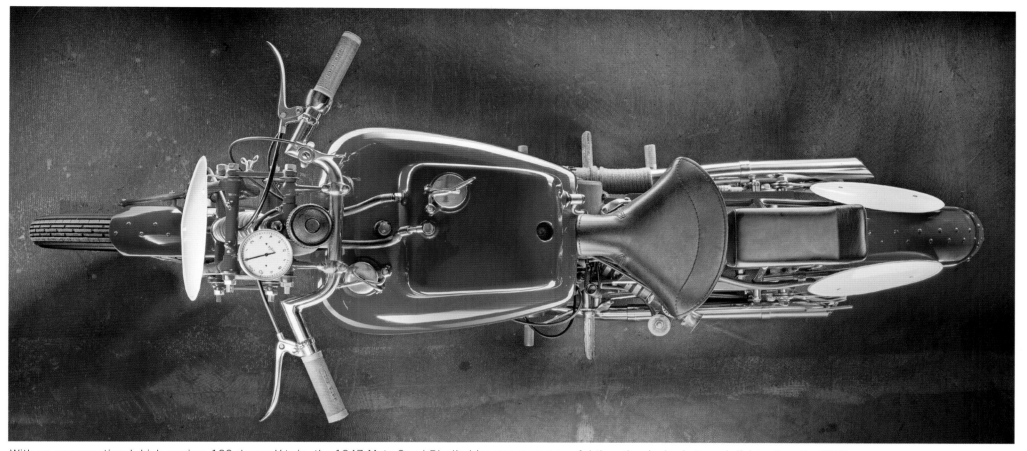

With an unconventional, high-revving, 120-degree V-twin, the 1947 Moto Guzzi Bicylindrica was more powerful than the singles but much lighter than the BMWs.

The ten years after the war were good for Italian motorcycle racing, and Guzzis racked up many wins with unique and expensive bikes. The company even built its own wind tunnel for testing and refinement of its machines, the first motorcycle manufacturer to do so. Unfortunately, this success was unsustainable. Citing the high costs associated with racing, in 1957 the company (along with Gilera and Mondial) abruptly pulled the plug on factory racing machines and the production spin-offs that resulted, and directed focus to street bikes. Thus began a short decline, which ended ten years later in full financial insolvency and a retreat into state ownership. The future of the company looked bleak.

Fortunately, Moto Guzzi's modern V-twins—jaw-dropping transverse, 45-degree, air-cooled

superbikes—arrived just in time for the firm to retain a slim but tenacious hold on the market that quickly became dominated by Japanese bikes. The first, an emblematic 700cc model meant to serve as a police bike, became the icon the company needed. The first civilian production bikes were the V-7s, which quickly evolved into the 850cc machines in the 1970s. With the engine placed sideways and crankshaft oriented longitudinally, blipping the throttle would cause the whole bike to twist beneath you like some reptilian monster. The lineup boasted an early system of linked brakes using three discs—an advanced design for the times.

When De Tomaso Industries bought the company in 1973, the new management didn't invest heavily in product development, but did capitalize on the unique

1947 MOTO GUZZI BICYLINDRICA SPECIFICATIONS:

Engine type:
Air-cooled SOHC V-twin

Displacement:
500 cubic centimeters

Horsepower:
NA

Special feature:
Unique 120-degrees V-twin engine known as the Bicylindrica.

Though this 250cc Moto Guzzi single was built in 1956, it remained competitive in racing for many years. Englishman John Kidson rode it to a sixth-place finish in the 1963 Isle of Man Lightweight TT 250cc class.

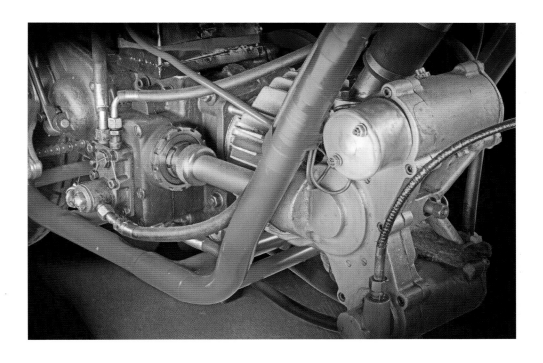

This double-overhead cam top end on this example was hand-crafted by Moto Guzzi factory racer Maurice Cann.

Below: Kidson credits his Isle of Man success aboard this motorcycle to the large gas tank, which allowed him to finish the race without having to stop to refuel.

design of the transverse V-twins. These distinctive bikes, with their lateral, upward-protruding cylinders, were sturdy, fast, and handled remarkably well. Beautiful and formidable, the machines were capable of competing, if not for racing glory or market share, at least for the admiration of the motorcycle enthusiasts who lusted after them.

But motorcycle manufacturing on a small scale is never easy and rarely profitable, so the company pulled up stakes and has reformed twice already since the De Tomaso Days. Acquired by Aprilia in 2000 and then Piaggio in 2004, the brand is still in business to this day. While production is fairly limited compared to the bigger manufacturers, this Italian heritage remains with beautiful, sexy bikes and a silhouette that is unmistakably Moto Guzzi.

1956 MOTO GUZZI 250 DOHC
SPECIFICATIONS:

Engine type:
Air-cooled, forward-facing
horizontal single cylinder

Displacement:
250 cubic centimeters

Horsepower:
NA

Special feature:
Rare small-capacity Moto Guzzi single
with near-vertical carburetor close
to the steering head.

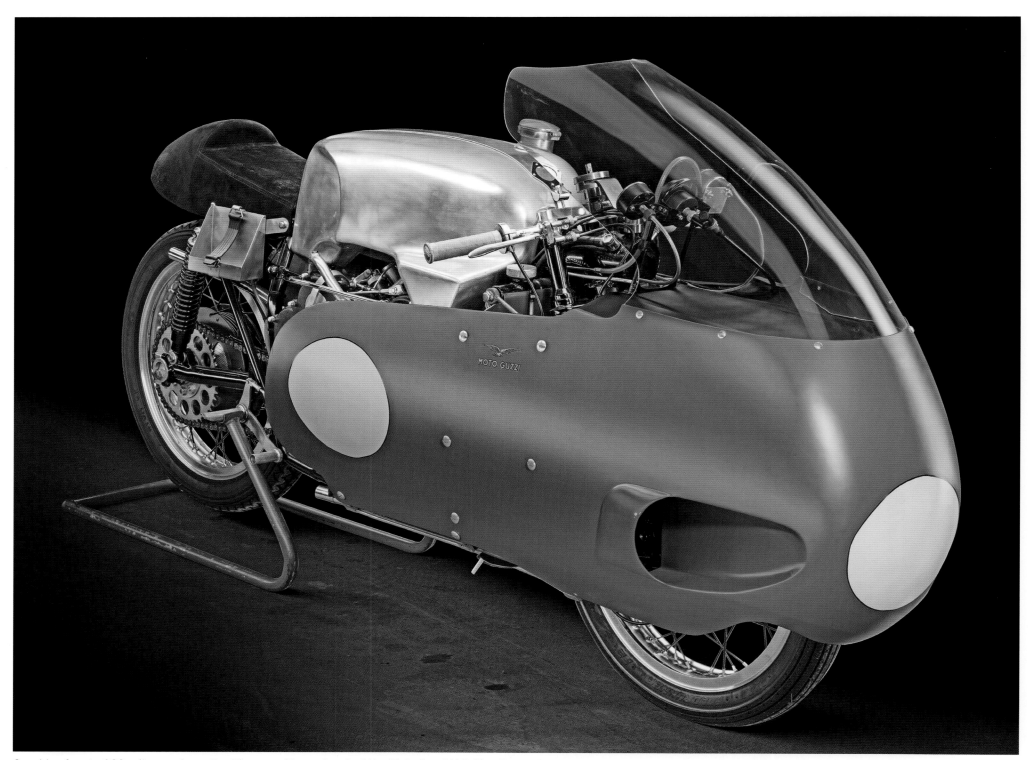

Capable of up to 180 miles per hour, the Discovery Channel ranked the Moto Guzzi V-8 "Otto" one of the ten most important motorcycles of all time.

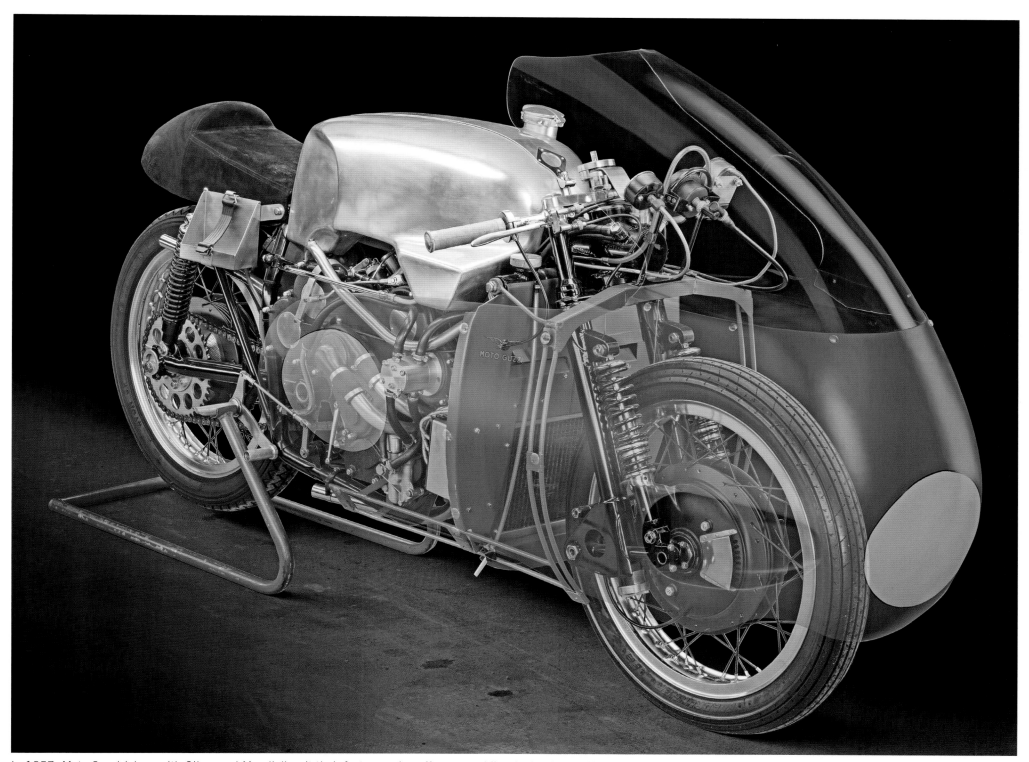

In 1957, Moto Guzzi (along with Gilera and Mondial) quit their factory racing effort—race bikes had to be cobbled together by privateers.

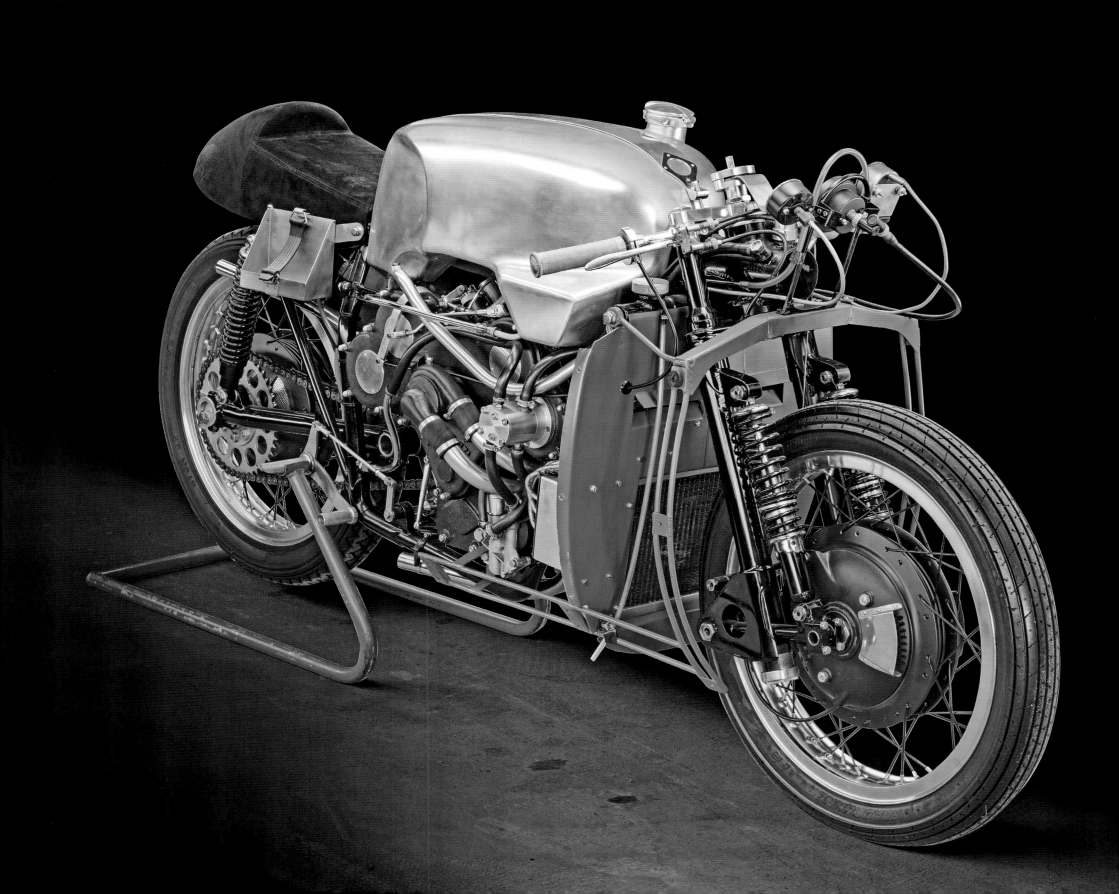

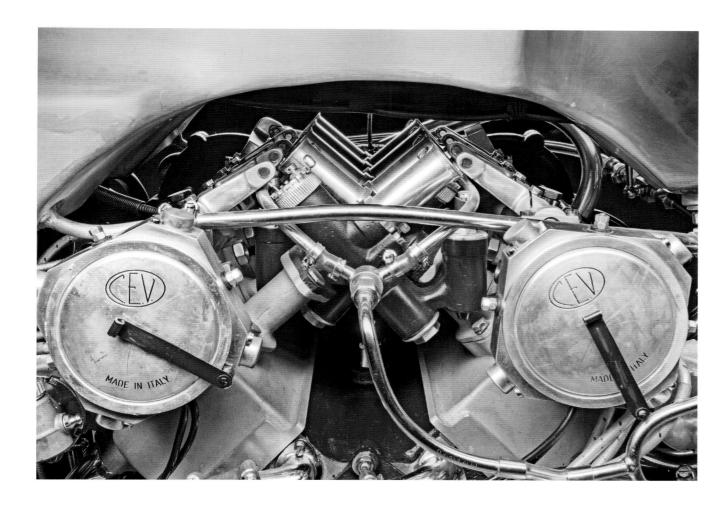

The water-cooled, 500cc, eight-cylinder Guzzi racer was meant to upend Grand Prix racing, but the bike proved to be nearly impossible to tune, unreliable, and practically unrideable.

Not the prettiest bike in the stable, the Moto Guzzi V-8 (called the "Otto") was built specifically for the Guzzi race team for the 1955 Grand Prix race season.

1955 MOTO GUZZI 500 V-8 REPLICA
SPECIFICATIONS:

Engine type:
Air-cooled DOHC across-the-frame 8-cylinder

Displacement:
499 cubic centimeters

Horsepower:
78

Special feature:
The fastest roadracing motorcycle
in the world in 1955.

CHAPTER II

1927 Henderson Four

The Henderson brothers got into the motorcycle business in Detroit, Michigan, in 1912. The motorcycles the brothers produced became known for endurance and distance races, as well as speed contests and hillclimbs. In 1917, Alan Bedell set a record by riding more than 1,100 miles on a California racetrack at an average speed of 48 miles an hour, then went on to break "Cannonball" Baker's time for the Los Angeles–to–New York run by making the trip in less than eight days, particularly inspiring considering the quality of rural roads at the time! Another formidable achievement aboard a Henderson Four was Carl Clancy's round-the-world trip. Starting in Dublin, Ireland, Clancy circumnavigated the globe, riding more than 15,000 miles in two years throughout Africa, Asia, Europe, and North America. In 1912.

In 1917, Schwinn Bicycles (which owned the Excelsior Motor Company) bought Henderson, and production was moved to Chicago, Illinois, and resumed under the Excelsior umbrella. Hendersons enjoyed a good export market and were popular rides in Europe and Australia. The 1920 Henderson K was the first production bike to use a fully pressurized oil lubrication system and an optional reverse gear (for Hendersons fitted with sidecars).

With powerful, reliable engines and the expert management and product development of Ignaz Schwinn, the Henderson marque could have been a long-term contender. Even when the US stock market crashed in 1929, Hendersons' sales remained strong, and the company competed head to head with Indian and Harley-Davidson for market dominance. But as the Great Depression worsened, in 1931 production of both Excelsior and Henderson motorcycles abruptly halted, as the parent company contracted to focus on its core business of building bicycles. Production of motorcycles in the Chicago factory never resumed.

A much-heralded (and expensive!) revival of the marque was attempted in the mid-1990s when Minnesota businessman and avid motorcyclist Dan Hanlon purchased the rights to the brand. The newly formed Excelsior-Henderson Motor Company produced a couple thousand Excelsior-Henderson Super X models, but the poorly managed company

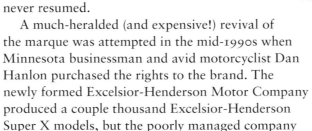

The 1927 Henderson Four was an inline four-cylinder with a long wheelbase that would become a Henderson trademark. Early models had folding hand cranks to start the motorcycle.

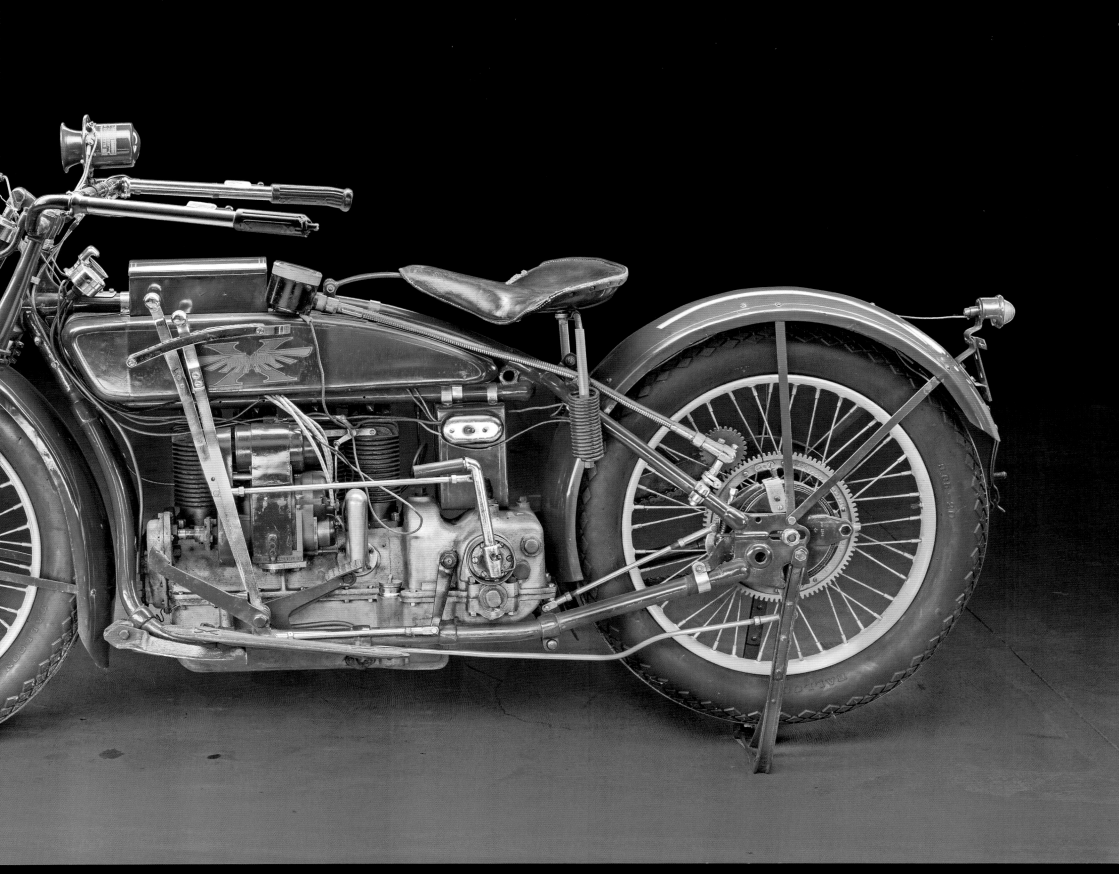

quickly failed and the marque was left once more to the history books.

The Henderson Four was an inline, four-cylinder engine with a long wheelbase that would become a Henderson trademark. Early models had a folding hand crank to start the motorcycle. Like other American manufacturers, the Hendersons were big bikes from the very beginning: The 1912 Four had a 900cc engine. The 1927 DeLuxe had a fancy instrument cluster with a speedometer, oil light, ammeter, and switch for the headlight. Because they were the fastest machines on the road at the time, Hendersons were popular for police work.

Like other American manufacturers, the Hendersons were big bikes from the very beginning. With their large displacements and heavy chassis, the bikes made great endurance racers.

Opposite page: The Henderson Four's 1,300cc side-valve engine could push the bike to nearly 100 miles per hour. Hendersons were popular for police work because they were the fastest machines on the road at the time.

1927 HENDERSON FOUR SPECIFICATIONS:

Engine type:
Air-cooled, in-line 4-cylinder

Displacement:
1,300 cubic centimeters

Horsepower:
35

Special feature:
The Henderson brothers were early pioneers of 4-cylinder motorcycles.

Henderson motorcycles were known for clever and careful attention to detail. A ring gear on the rear hub drove a tiny pinion gear connected to a speedometer.

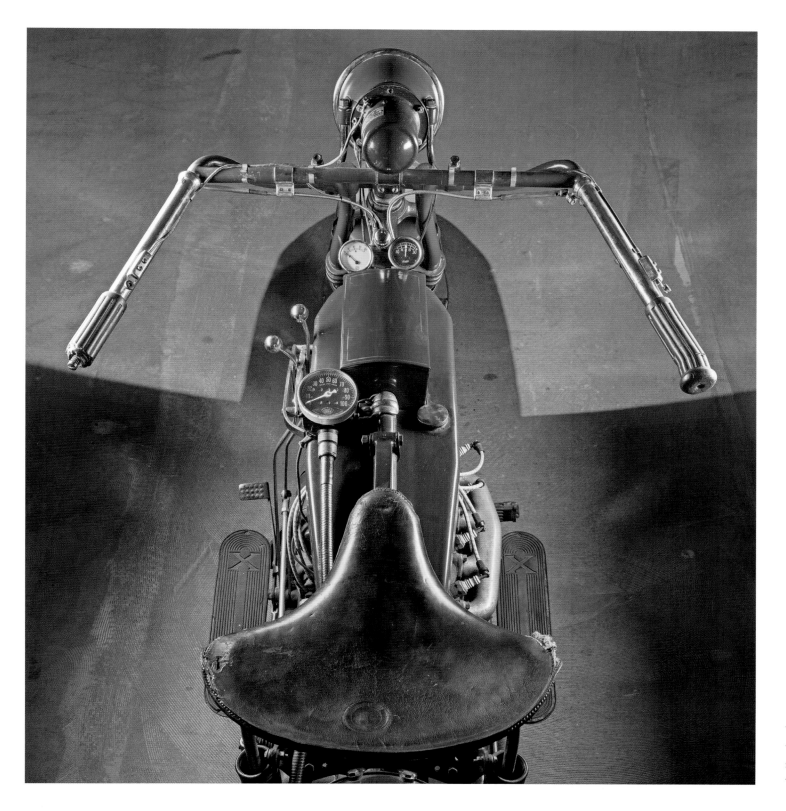

The 1927 Henderson had a fancy and functional instrument cluster with a speedometer, oil light, ammeter, and switch for the headight.

CHAPTER 12

1928 Neander

Ernst Neumann-Neander founded the Neander Motorfahrzeug (motor vehicle) in Duren, Germany, in 1926. As a young man, Neumann had an active interest in steam engine technology, bicycles, and racing, so it's little surprise that his enthusiasm led him in the direction of the newest European craze in personal mobility: the motorcycle.

In 1924 Neander won a medal for a prototype motorcycle design at the Deutschlandfahrt Rally in Germany. The concept of automobility—driving machines for the common man—became his passion. He added Neumann ("new man") to his last name and began designing vehicles based on practicality, comfort, and ergonomic principles.

His first production model, the Tourist, used a central spinal steel-tube frame. He went quickly on to create the P1, a much more unique design in which the frame was built from an I-beam forged in a U shape—one of the earliest examples of the twin-spar frame used on sport bikes today. While not groundbreaking by today's standards, it was a totally new concept in the 1920s. The construction technique was also known in the art world from, of all places, the Eiffel Tower in France, which used a similar type of design for the support structure. Neander later created a very strong, very fast race bike based on the P1 with a 175cc engine that weighed only 90 pounds.

Another unique feature of the P1, and many of the Neander machines to follow, was that it was built from a metal called duralumin. Given the name because a company based in Duren built it, duralumin was an aluminum alloy with a composition that included copper, magnesium, and manganese. Due to its strength and light weight, duralumin was popular in the aircraft industry for use in rigid framing structures, including those used in the German Zeppelins and US Navy airships. The material was also, as Neander found out, ideal for the monocoque frame construction that made for some remarkable motorcycles, both long ago and recently. Because of duralumin's propensity for oxidization, surfaces were plated with cadmium.

Neander's frames were constructed in a way that made production simple and easy, and the company was able to produce a complete motorcycle in only half a day. The P1 and future bikes such as the P3 and racing machines used Villiers, JAP, and MAG engines up to 1,000cc to keep the production process simple and the machines reliable.

Aside from a limited production run of nearly two thousand motorcycles in the late 1920s, Neumann-Neander mostly limited its efforts to hand-built, one-off vehicles—sometimes featuring two wheels, sometimes three, sometimes four. One of the most interesting and compelling Neander vehicles was a three-wheel racer in which the chassis remained perpendicular to the road (or, parallel, if you prefer) while the wheels angled into the turns.

The 1928 Neander was made from a box-section, duralumin frame, and had a pivoting front fork. Opel licensed the design and continued to build roadsters and racers for a few years before quitting.

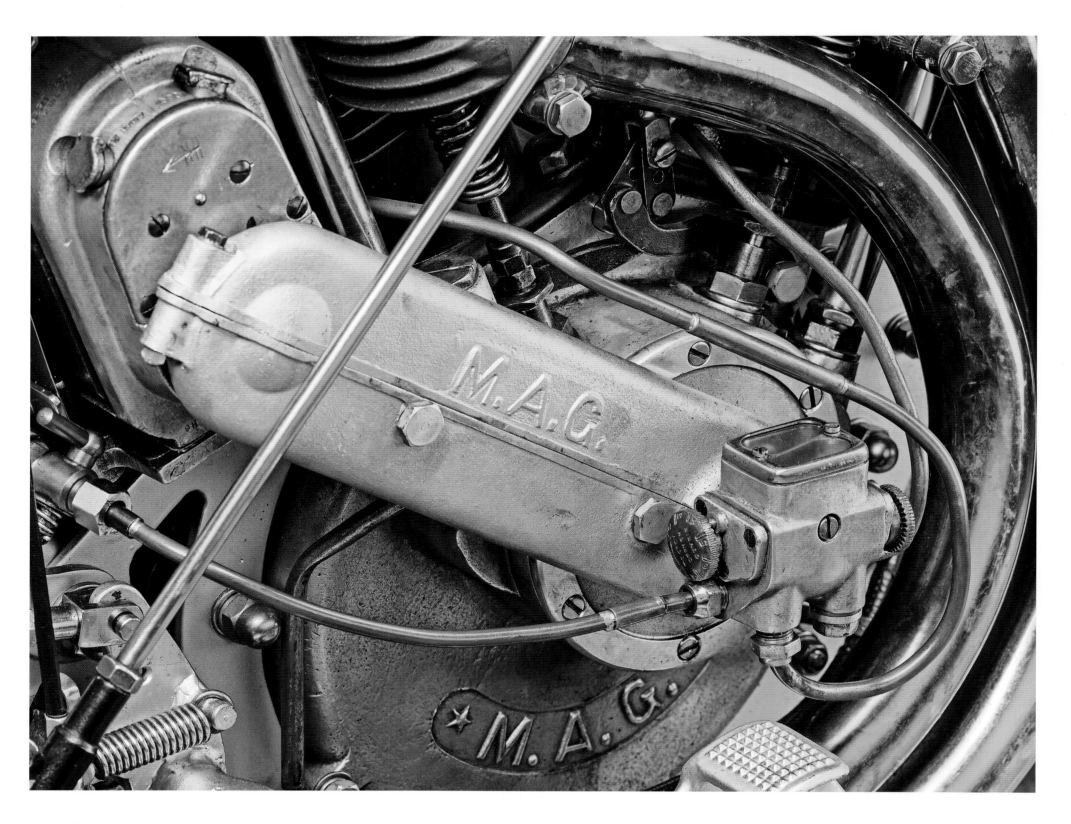

Fit, finish, and attention to detail made the 1928 Neander a lovely machine. Ernst Neumann-Neander is remembered more as an avant-garde artist than motorcycle builder.

Left: Neander motorcycles used JAP, Villiers, and MAG engines to keep the production process simple. Neanders could be built at a rate of one to two per day.

1928 NEANDER SPECIFICATIONS:

Engine type:
Air-cooled V-twin

Displacement:
NA

Horsepower:
NA

Special feature:
This bike was restored using dull aluminum paint to replace the original cadmium plating because of German environmental regulations.

CHAPTER 13

1929 Harley-Davidson JDH and 1975 XR750

Harley-Davidson is the poster child for long-term motorcycle success. Like BMW, Moto Guzzi, and Triumph, the company spent the twentieth century steadfastly churning out predictable, satisfying rides, never deviating too far from a core design or trademark feature, and clinging tenaciously to tradition even when every indicator in the market pointed a different direction. Harley-Davidson discovered a winning combination of a powerful, unmistakable V-twin engine in a chassis that could soak up the vast, straight-line distances of rural America.

Arguably the world's most famous motorcycle manufacturer, Harley-Davidson began its story in a backyard shed in Milwaukee, Wisconsin, in 1902. Arthur Davidson and his friend William Harley built a 400cc single, then mounted it to a bicycle with the help of Davidson's brothers Walter and William. After a couple years of trial and error, improving the engine's performance and strengthening its frame, Harley-Davidson acquired a small factory (located where the current headquarters now resides)

Continued on page 81

Between World War I and World War II, the standard Harley-Davidson paint finish was a gloss olive drab with pinstripe accents, a nod to the doughboys returning home and looking for adventure.

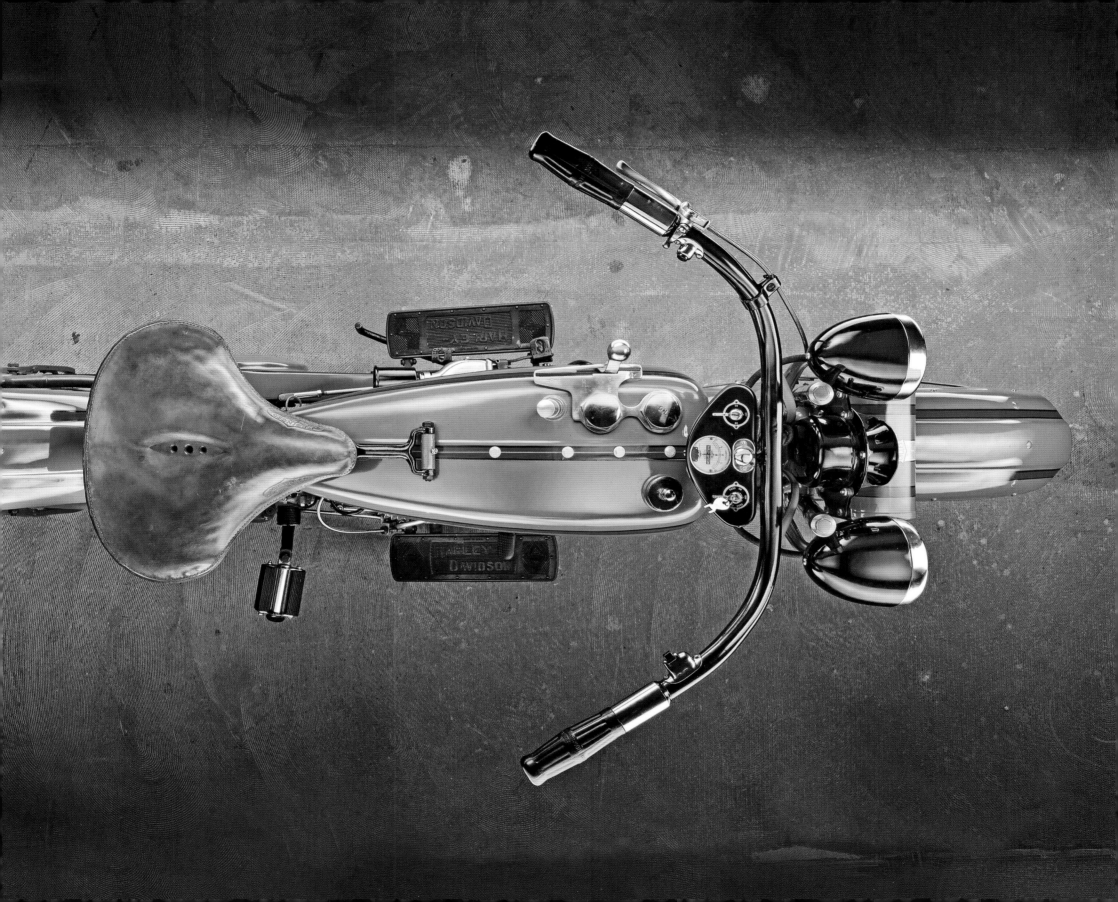

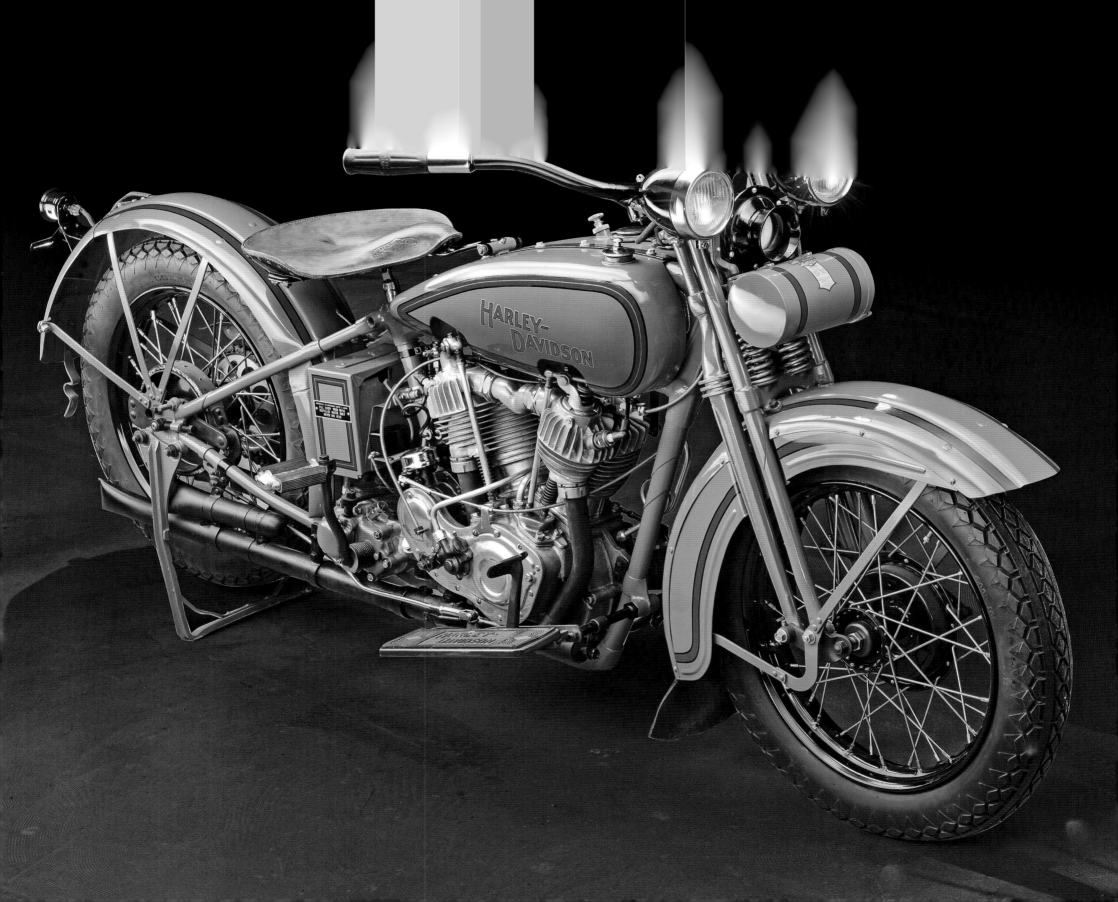

Above: The Harley-Davidson factory was well established by 1929 and took great care in appointing even the boring details of motorcycle design, including a pinstriped battery box.

Left: Up until 1929, Harley-Davidsons were intended primarily for transportation. Sporting riders preferred Indian Scouts, Super X twins, or Henderson Fours, so Harley built the JDH to compete.

Continued from page 76

and began small-scale production. In addition to civilians, the company was selling bikes to police departments, establishing a customer base that continues today.

Right away, in true American tradition, the quest for more power and more speed led the company to start making bigger bikes. Some fits and starts with bigger singles didn't pan out, so Harley turned to twins. By 1913, Harley was massproducing the Model 9E with a 45-degree, 1,000cc twin that only produced 10 horsepower with a modern frame, leading link forks, no rear suspension, and chain final drive.

Big on displacement and low on power is the Harley-Davidson tradition; these simple designs feature unforgettable looks, pulse-quickening sound, and that oh-so-satisfying big-twin feel. Harley-Davidson survived the arrival and success of the Ford Model T that drove many other motorcycle manufacturers out of business.

While it's best known for its bigger motorcycles, the Milwaukee company achieved great racing success with a smaller 750cc (45-cubic-inch) twin, the model W. Demand for the "forty-fives" (cubic inches) boomed during World War II, during which Harley produced more than ninety thousand WLA models for the American and Allied military.

Harley-Davidson introduced the model 61E in 1936. It was a 1,000cc overhead valve V-twin also known as a knucklehead. All future big-bore Harleys can be traced back to this one ancestor. Later bikes with novel new features also got cool nicknames, such as the Hydra Glide in 1949, which sported a hydraulically damped front suspension; the Duo Glide in 1958 that featured rear suspension components; and the Electra Glide in 1965, which introduced an electric starting mechanism to the zillions of Harley enthusiasts who had finally gotten good at kick starting their beasts to life. Engine size grew too, to

The engine was a 1,200cc, 45-degree, air-cooled twin using inlet-over-exhaust valves to send 29 horsepower to the ground.

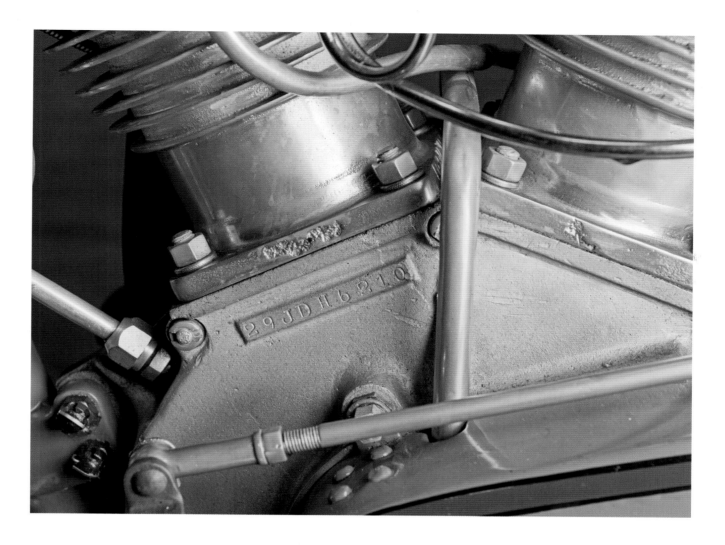

The stamped VIN on the 1929 Harley-Davidson JDH. By 1927, the company was selling nearly twenty thousand bikes per year. The JDH was meant to be a sporting model.

1,200cc just after World War II, and then to 1,340cc in the late 1970s. Rubber mounts were given to the engines for a smoother vibration, and wind-cheating fairings and luggage became popular options for long-haul travel.

Probably the most famous of Harley-Davidson bikes was the FL Hydra-Glide, introduced in 1949, a

Continued on page 85

1929 HARLEY-DAVIDSON JDH SPECIFICATIONS:

Engine type:
Air-cooled V-twin

Displacement:
1,207 cubic centimeters

Horsepower:
29

Special feature:
Upright generator parallel to the front cylinder led to the nickname "Three Cylinder."

Above: The low center of gravity and smooth power delivery of the 1975 Harley-Davidson XR750 racers has made them the dominant force on the dirt tracks for over forty years.

Left: What does it take to build a Harley that can win races? A modified Sportster with Italian forks and wheels, Japanese carburetors, no brakes, and a mile-long dirt oval.

Continued from page 81

motorcycle that represents the archetype of classic American iron. The FL inspired all future cruisers and dressers, both within the Motor Company and halfway across the world, when the Japanese copied the idea and started selling metric cruisers. The FL frame appeared nearly ten years prior, and the panhead engine the year before, but the real step forward for the Hydra-Glide was the hydraulic telescopic fork, which had twice the suspension travel of the previous girder ("springer") fork but held the road much better, and looked cleaner as well. The front end used a big fender, massive fork legs, and a big fuel tank, giving the bike that quintessential broad-shouldered appearance that remains on big cruisers today.

Harley-Davidson introduced the 883 Sportster in 1957. Noticeably smaller and somewhat lighter than its bigger brothers, they made great racers on dirt and flat tracks, dominating speedway competition ever since. These bikes, eventually offered also as 1,200cc models, were hugely popular, simple, fun bikes to ride. Nowadays, using modern suspension technology and Evolution engines, the Sportster is one of the best-selling motorcycles in the United States.

Harley-Davidson hit tough times in the late 1960s and 1970s, as more and more Americans turned to reliable, imported motorcycles with more positive power-to-weight ratios. The company was in trouble and bought out by American Machine and Foundry (AMF—the bowling ball people) in 1969, which then tried to drive the Harley name into the toilet. Quality, reliability, handing, and performance all declined as AMF ramped up production in order to extract every cent of profit from the division it viewed as nothing but a cash cow.

Much of the damage done to Harley-Davidson during this time was mitigated by the efforts of Willie G. Davidson, grandson of Harley-Davidson founder

Harley's most prized competition machine, the XR750 was the weapon of choice for race legends Mark Brelsford, Randy Goss, Cal Rayborn, and Jay Springsteen.

William Davidson. Willie G., as he is known, was primarily responsible for approving new Harley-Davidson designs from the mid-1960s onward. But he also applied his design talents to create several memorable Harley-Davidson motorcycles. The grandson Davidson is remembered for shaking up the status quo at Harley's design studio with deviations from traditional ideas that ultimately helped save the company. At first, Davidson's ideas were considered too radical and impractical for the well-established marque, but steady pressure and sound ideas eventually paid off. His first victory for the evolution of the company was the Super Glide, Harley's first attempt at a factory custom, a production bike with design flourishes similar to what a customer could get in a small fabrication or customization shop, such as a raked-out chopper or boulevard cruiser.

1975 HARLEY-DAVIDSON XR750
SPECIFICATIONS:

Engine type:
Air-cooled OHV V-twin

Displacement:
748 cubic centimeters

Horsepower:
82

Special feature:
These bikes featured Italian wheels and front forks and Japanese-made carburetors.

PART II

Finding the Groove

By the time the Great Depression laid waste to the motorcycle (and virtually every other) industry, the basic template for the motorcycle had been established. Details great and small would change—overhead valves, often operated by overhead cams, would replace side valves and inlet-over-exhaust valves, telescopic forks would replace sprung girder forks in performing suspension duties in the front, while in the rear swinging arm rear suspensions would replace, well, nothing, since there were no rear suspensions on early bikes—but the basic layout had been established. The motorcycle essentially retained the shape of the safety bicycle upon which it had been based, with the engine mounted in the V formed by the frame tubes and a gas tank straddling the top frame tube, a seat would be placed behind the gas tank, and the rider would operate the machine by a variety of hand and foot pedals and levers and steer the whole thing via a handlebar mounted to the front fork.

But this period was anything but boring, due in large part to the vibrant motorcycle racing scene that flourished. This was a golden age of motorcycle racing around the world. In Europe the great Grand Prix circus traveled Gypsy-like from one of the world's great racing circuits and road courses to the next, and in the United States, riders battled each other on dirt ovals, often converted horse racetracks, and on TT courses.

Because of this emphasis on racing, motorcycle performance made huge advances during this period. The basic design might have been settled, but this was the age of craftsman tuners who could work their magic on relatively stock motorcycles, coaxing from them levels of performance that would have been unimaginable to riders of pedestrian versions of those same motorcycles.

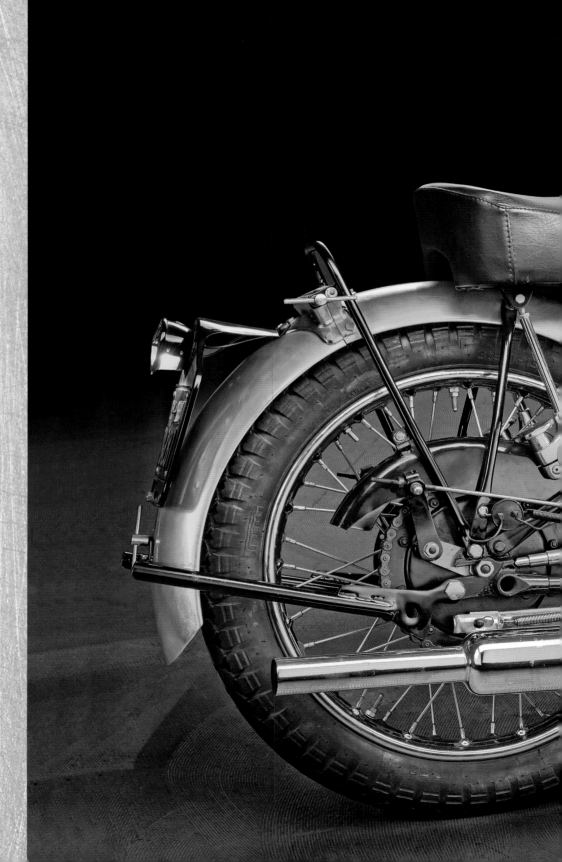

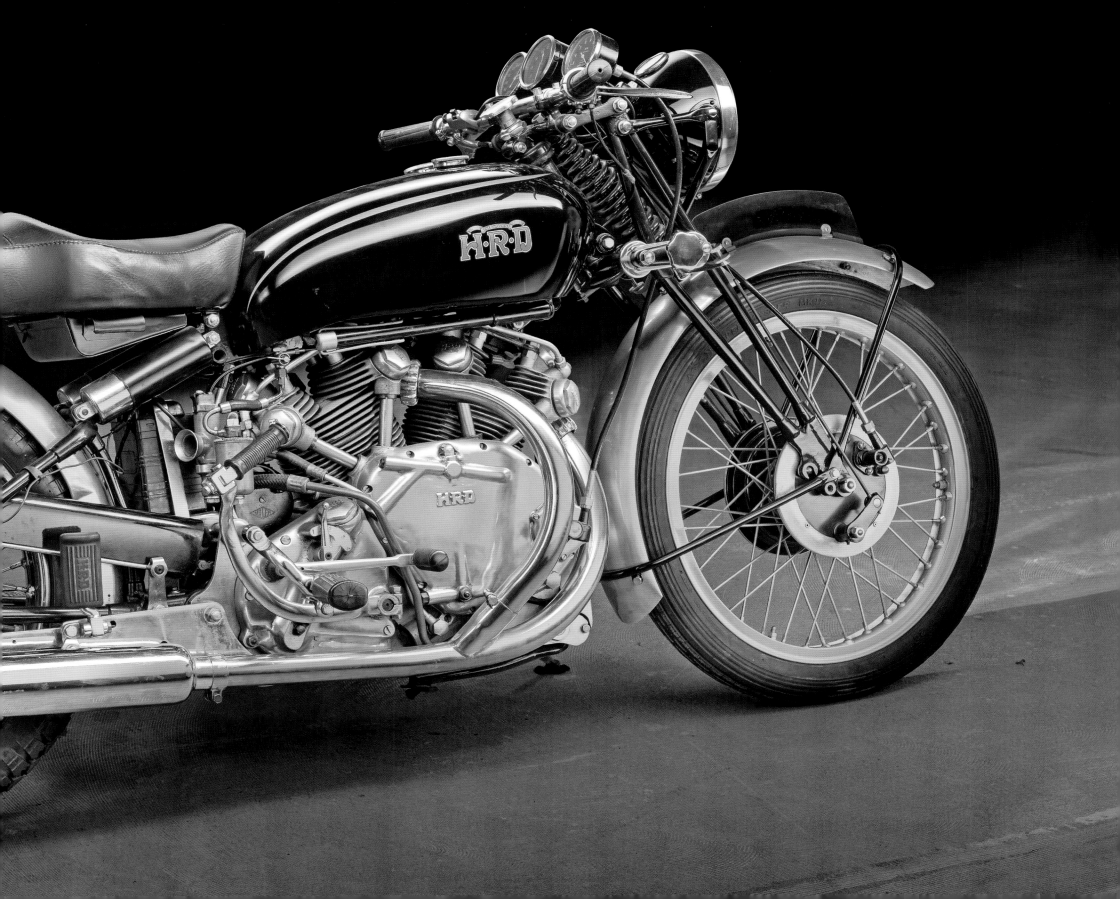

CHAPTER 14

1929 Norton CS1

Founded in 1898 in Birmingham, England, Norton began producing motorcycles using imported engines in 1902. Interest and success in racing came early for Norton, and racing guided the development of its motorcycles for sixty years. A year after a class win with a Peugeot engine at the very first Isle of Man TT in 1907, the firm began manufacturing bikes for the public using their own engines. The early bikes were mostly 500cc models, but included the nearly 650cc "Big Four," a great fit for sidecar duty. These bikes set numerous speed records before World War I.

Nortons dominated European racing, consistently winning Grand Prix and TT races in multiple categories through the 1930s. These machines quickly became known as some of the best-handling bikes ever built. While racing halted during the wars, the export and manufacturing of military motorcycles helped ensure the company maintained its status. Norton supplied one hundred thousand motorcycles to the military during World War II, nearly a quarter of the Allies' motorcycle fleet, which left it positioned as a strong market competitor after the war.

In the years following World War II, Norton reached its apex, winning races hand over fist and producing some of its most cherished designs. Norton won the junior and senior TT classes four years in a row, from 1950 to 1953, a feat second only to MV Agusta's TT wins that came in the later 1950s and 1960s. Introduced in this time period were the Dominator twin (1949), the featherbed frame (1950), and the Commando (1967).

It is hard to overstate the significance of Norton's engineering feats during this time. The featherbed frame propelled Norton's fame for decades by providing the best road-holding ability known to motorcycles at the time. The Commando, with an Isolastic frame that reduced the vibration of the big twin, was so fast, held the road so well, and was so popular that the company went on to produce a half million of them over the next ten years. Predating the Honda CB750, the Commando was really the world's first production superbike. It was only Norton's low production numbers and constant flirtation with financial collapse that prevented it from being the bike that changed motorcycling in the late '60s.

Unfortunately, the competition from Japan proved to be too much for Norton. The speed and tradition of bikes made in the United Kingdom weren't enough to overcome the fact that Japanese bikes, while perhaps lacking that British charm, were just as fast, cheaper, and more reliable. Like Triumph, the company went through periods of hope and decline, joining with BSA and Triumph for a short time to form Norton-Villiers-Triumph. For fifteen years Norton kept swinging away with new models in hopes of another big hit, but ultimately failed to capture the glory of the postwar years.

In its final years, Norton plodded on and achieved some modest success producing bikes with rotary engines, but the small production numbers kept prices too high to generate much market success and the factory went dormant.

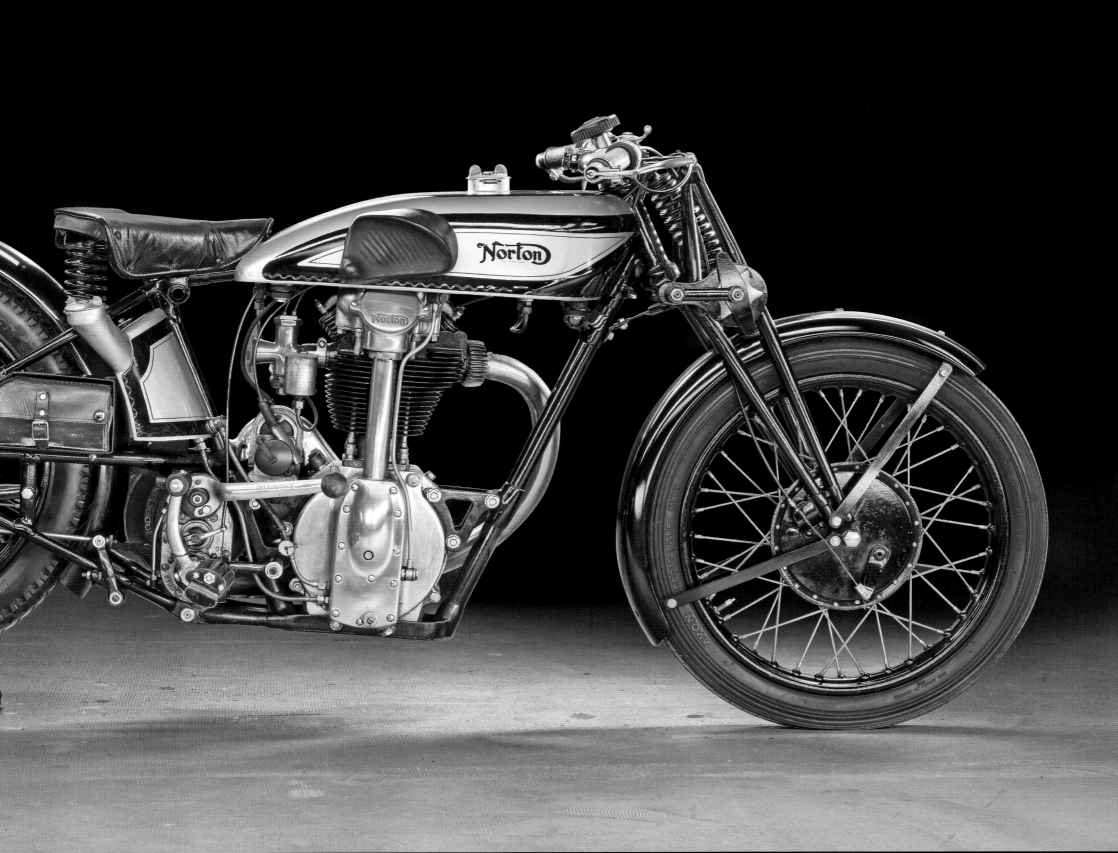

Previous pages: The bike Che Guevara was said to have ridden around much of South America was a 16H Norton, a predecessor to this one, the 1927 Norton Model 18.

Left: The Model 18 sported a 500cc, overhead-valve single, and is believed to carry the largest flat tank ever affixed to a Norton. In true racing form, the tank has a TT filler cap and top vent.

1929 NORTON CS1 SPECIFICATIONS:

Engine type:
Air-cooled, SOHC single cylinder

Displacement:
490 cubic centimeters

Horsepower:
25

Special feature:
Right-side hand shift gearbox lever, nicknamed the "cricket bat motor."

CHAPTER 15

Circa 1925 Rudge

Rudge-Whitworth was created through the merger of two bicycle manufacturers of the same name. Rudge motorcycles were produced from 1911 to 1946, with a narrow range of engine sizes of 250–500cc. Rudge-Whitworth was known for its early adoption of four-valve cylinder heads.

The Rudge Ulster was a 500cc four-valve single with overhead valves, and it was one of the earliest examples of a linked braking system, in which the brake pedal controlled both front and rear brakes, while the hand lever controlled only the front. The Special was a touring bike; the Ulster was a sport bike.

Early Rudge bikes, like the Rudge Multi (gear), were famous for a using a clever belt-drive transmission that was self-tensioning—an early example of the modern continuously variable transmission (CVT) that offered up to twenty-one forward gear ratios. After a notable win at the Ulster Grand Prix race with an average speed of more than 80 miles per hour, the sporty Rudge Ulster was produced to allow everyday riders to capture some of the glory—an early version of the race-replica bike. These lightweight machines were supremely agile, stopped rather well, and were capable of more than 100 miles per hour from their small overhead cam, four-valve singles. Some smaller Rudge-Whitworth bikes won early Isle of Man TT junior and senior class events.

Like many motorcycle manufacturers that failed around the time of the Great Depression, Rudge-Whitworth fell victim to financial troubles. After several notable and energizing racing successes in the 1920s, sales and profits fell in the 1930s. A brief revival of the marque came in the late 1930s at the hands of a new owner, but the outbreak of World War II dictated that the company focus all its production on a necessary and profitable military need: the manufacture of radar and communications equipment. Production of these remarkable bikes never resumed.

While it looked big and heavy, the Rudge was actually a lightweight bike, capable of well over eighty miles per hour.

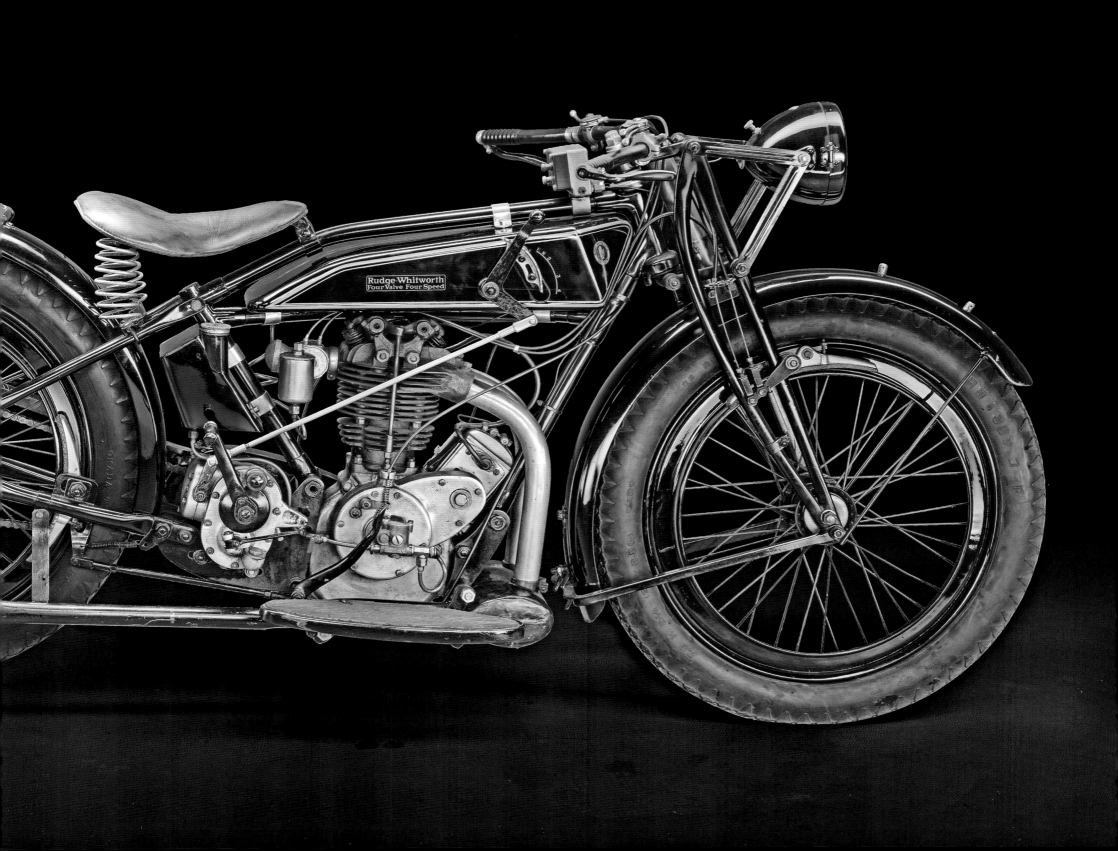

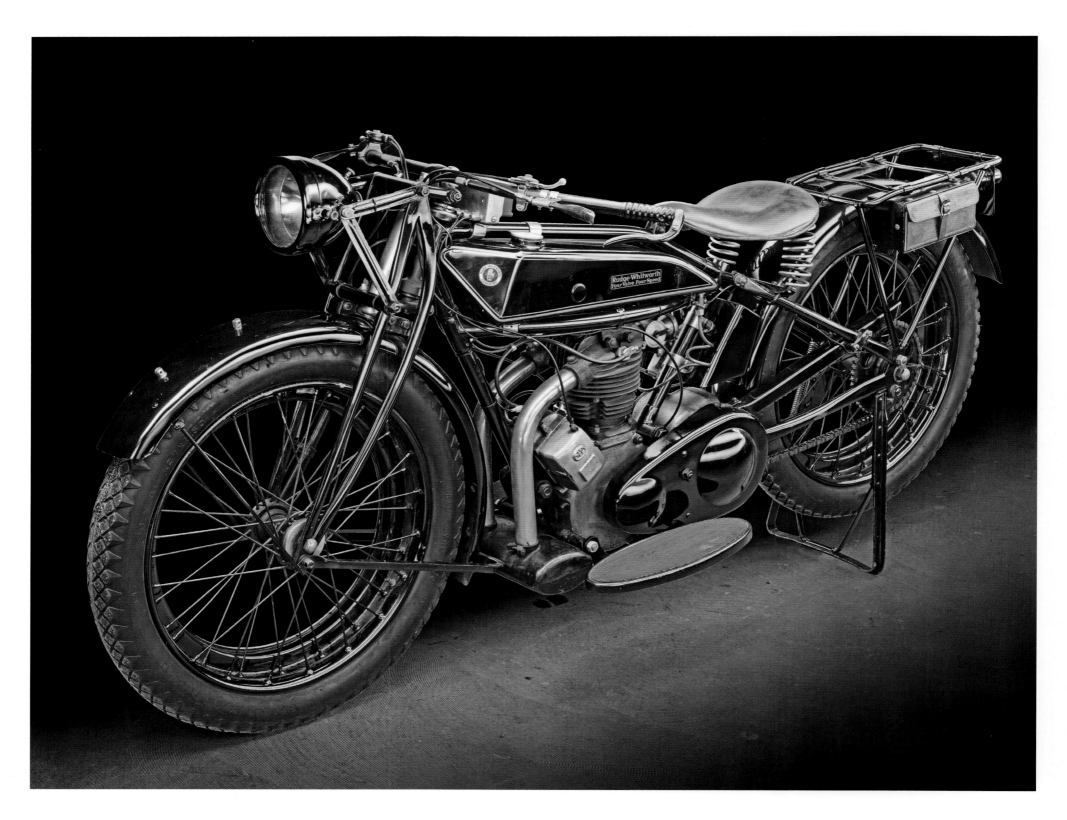

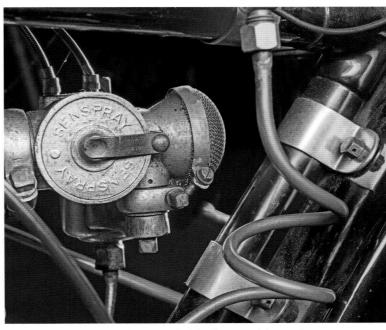

The 500cc Rudge Multi was named for its use of four-valves per cylinder, not because of the number of cylinders. Rudge was among the first to incorporate a four-valve design.

The 500cc Rudge was available in a touring or a sports version. Both had four speeds and deployed both front and rear brakes, operated by the rider's foot.

Left: Rudge-Whitworth produced a fine array of motorcycles from 1911 to 1946. The company was known for clever engine and transmission designs, and its marketing pitch was "Rudge it, do not trudge it."

CIRCA 1925 RUDGE FOUR "MULTI"
SPECIFICATIONS:

Engine type:
Air-cooled, OHV single

Displacement:
500 cubic centimeters

Horsepower:
NA

Special feature:
High-quality, traditional British
do-everything motorcycle: Four, or Multi,
for 4-valves and 4-speeds.

CHAPTER 16

1932 Brough Superior

The Brough factory in Nottingham, England, outsourced production of much of their motorcycle components, including the engine, gearbox, and forks, and then assembled them one at a time for wealthy customers. Only a few thousand of these bikes were built over a twenty-year period (production was three or four a week, on average), and no two were ever truly alike. These bikes commanded a premium price few could afford and continue to do so today. Well-preserved SS80 and SS100 motorcycles can sell for hundreds of thousands of dollars at auction.

World War I British Army officer, archaeologist, and diplomat T. E. Lawrence (Lawrence of Arabia) was a huge fan of the marque, owning seven larger (1,000cc) versions of the SS during a long and illustrious run toward motorcyclist fame. In fact, Lawrence met his end at the early age of forty-six from a crash on his SS100. Lawrence's death prompted one of his physicians to begin studying motorcyclist injury and head trauma patterns and eventually led to the earliest pushes for protective headgear for both military and civilian motorcyclists.

Branded the Rolls-Royce of motorcycles by the enthusiast press, these bikes were relatively exclusive and terribly expensive for the time. And boy, were they fast—the paperwork from the factory "guaranteed" the bike could reach 100 miles per hour. The reliable and powerful V-twins with exposed valve gear combined with the curves, chrome, and length of the Brough designs made what many thought to be the best bikes ever built. They certainly were some of the most beautiful.

Handcrafted, these bikes were assembled twice: once to fit all the parts together and smooth out any rough edges, and again after the parts were painted, chromed, or polished. Each bike was test ridden and certified, ensuring they were up to Brough standards and design specifications. If a bike could not reach its guaranteed speed (100 miles per hour for the SS100 models), it was sent back to the factory to be reworked and remained there until it could perform as advertised.

The weight and length of these bikes gave them legendary stability and comfort at high speeds, but their ability to maneuver suffered for it—they were not a bike built for tight curves. The motorcycles made a name for themselves with several race wins and early land speed records. The Brough factory also built high-quality sidecars and one-of-a-kind automobiles in its short history.

Over a period of about twenty years, Brough produced about one motorcycle a day—these were exclusive, expensive machines built essentially by hand.

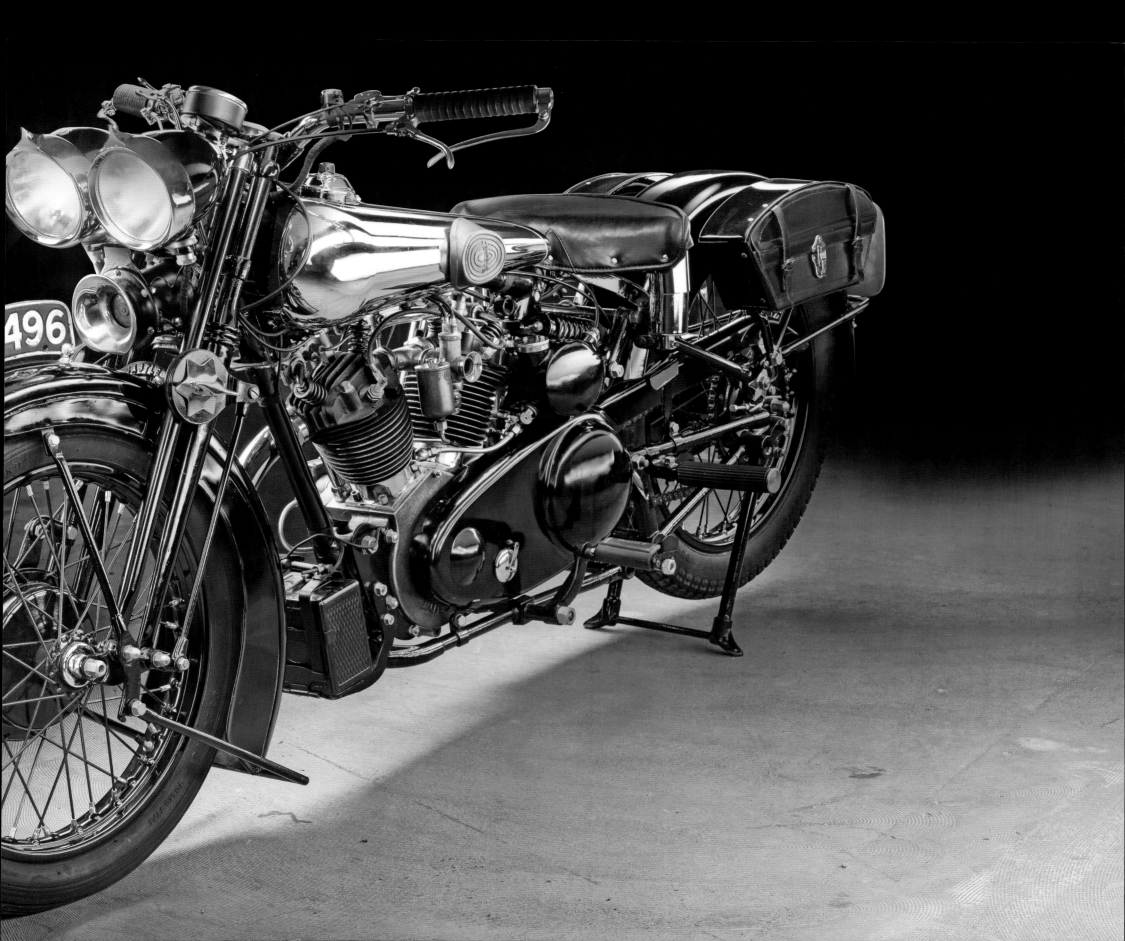

The Brough Superiors were considered the finest motorcycles built at the time. The Black Alpine (680cc) pictured here reduced the price somewhat, but was still finely appointed and expensive.

1932 BROUGH SUPERIOR BLACK ALPINE 680 SPECIFICATIONS:

Engine type:
Air-cooled, OHV V-twin manufactured by JAP

Displacement:
676 cubic centimeters

Horsepower:
NA

Special feature:
Broughs were custom-made by hand to order so no two were exactly the same.

CHAPTER 17

1933 Matchless Silver Hawk 4 and 1960 G50

Originating in London, England, in 1899 and existing until the late 1960s under various owners, including, late in life, the Norton-Villiers group, Matchless motorcycles had a long and complicated run. In 1931 Matchless acquired AJS motorcycles to form the Associated Motor Cycles (AMC) group and produced the same or similar bikes under both the Matchless and AJS badges—the same way General Motors produces similar vehicles under the Chevrolet and GMC badges.

One of the earliest Matchless bikes, piloted by the founder's son Charlie Collier, won the first Isle of Man TT singles race in 1907. Early Matchless singles were successful racers, but attempts to produce twins and fours held little commercial value in the motorcycle market. Some of their engines, however, lived on to power Brough Superior motorcycles and some other types of vehicles, such as the three-wheeled Morgan cars. The Silver Hawk was beautiful and well designed. But it was an over-engineered touring bike, released too close in proximity to the lean Depression years and the release of the Squariel, both of which quickly rendered it obsolete.

The limited run of the Silver Hawks was forced to compete for sales with the Ariel Square Four, which was lighter, smaller, cleaner looking, and easy to ride.

In the late 1930s, the company produced the G3L, a small, reliable single with a hydraulic, telescopic fork for the British military effort. The hydraulically damped telescopic fork first graced the military machines and then was used on all later Matchless models, becoming the default type of front suspension for nearly every motorcycle thereafter produced, anywhere in the world. After the war, AMC continued to produce reliable and trustworthy Matchless bikes for the government. These singles were also repurposed for civilian use, and Matchless began gaining in popularity. Through the twenty years following World War II, Matchless and AJS bikes provided some honest competition to bikes such as the Norton Manx, which were more powerful but less agile.

Instead of the skinny and wraithlike profiles of the 1910s and 1920s, the bikes of the 1930s began to develop a more barrel-chested, muscular look.

Arguably the most famous of Matchless models, the G50 was a demon on the track. With an air-cooled, two-valve 500cc single, these little racers came in at less than 300 pounds with 50-plus horsepower motors capable of speeds up to 135 miles per hour. The simplicity of the design helped the G50 even up with the more elaborate, heavier, and more powerful Norton Manx. Even after AMC failed, the Matchless name rights were sold and the bike lived on for another ten years as the Seeley G50, a four-stroke single.

While these bikes were terrific on the racetrack, AMC was getting spanked in the market by BSA. Shortly after AMC was taken over by the Norton-Villiers group, the limited popularity of Matchless and AJS bikes compared to Nortons and Triumphs meant the end for these remarkable machines. When AMC failed in the late 1960s, it took the names Matchless and AJS with it.

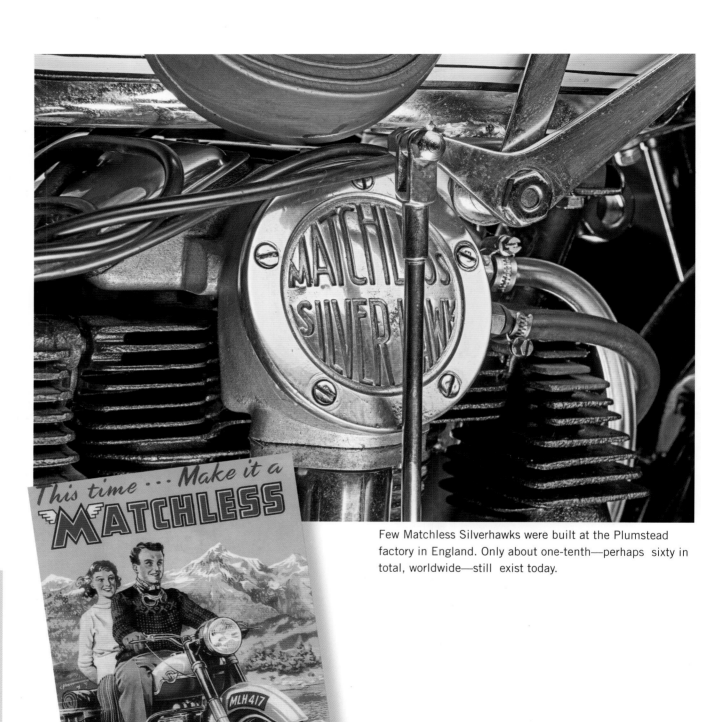

Few Matchless Silverhawks were built at the Plumstead factory in England. Only about one-tenth—perhaps sixty in total, worldwide—still exist today.

1933 MATCHLESS SILVER HAWK 4 SPECIFICATIONS:

Engine type:
Air-cooled SOHC V-four

Displacement:
592 cubic centimeters

Horsepower:
NA

Special feature:
The narrow-angle (26-degree) V-four engine featured a one-piece "monoblock" design and a single cylinder head for all four cylinders.

Opposite page: Designer Bert Collier described the Silver Hawk as a fascinating machine that "combines the silence, smoothness, and comfort of the most expensive motor car with a super-sports performance."

The big tank, sculpted seat, see-through chassis, megaphone exhaust, and exposed drivetrain of the 1960 Matchless G50 dare you to look away.

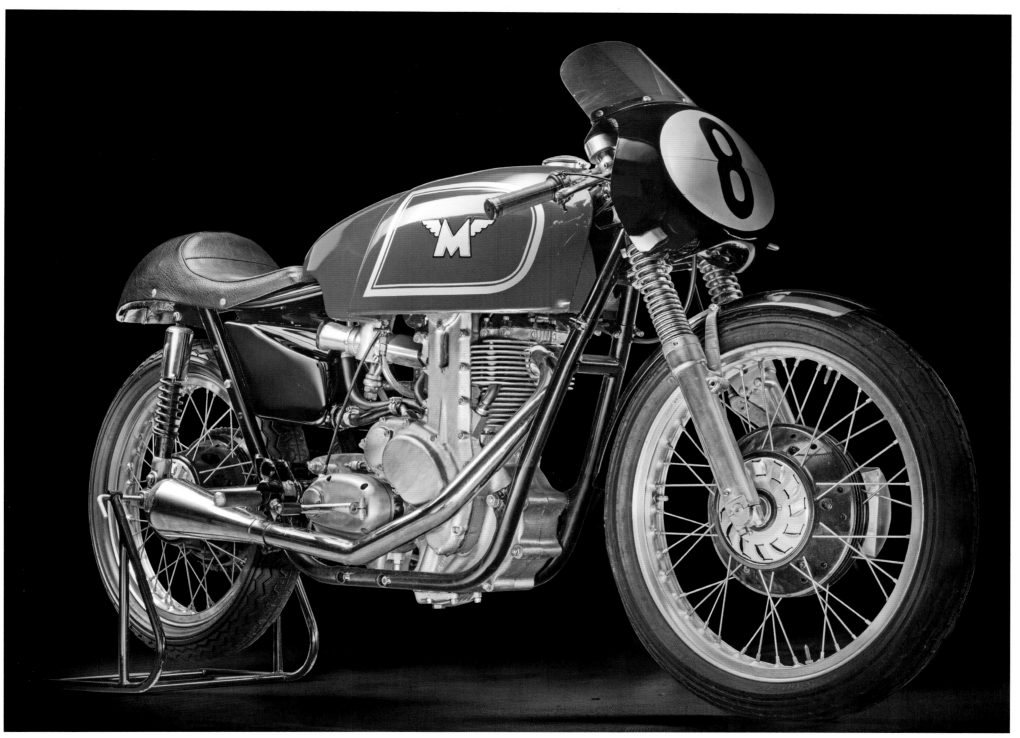

Lightweight, agile, and fast, the two-valve 500cc singles made 50 horsepower in a package of about 300 pounds. The simplicity of the design helped the G50 compete with the more powerful Norton Manx.

During the 1964 Grand Prix race season, Phil Read took podium finishes on a Matchless G50 in the United States, Belgium, and Germany.

1960 MATCHLESS G50 SPECIFICATIONS:

Engine type:
Air-cooled, SOHC single

Displacement:
496 cubic centimeters

Horsepower:
50

Special feature:
Handsome production racing motorcycle based on the 350 AJS 7R that was competitive with the Norton Manx.

It is not difficult to see how the Matchless version of this AMC bike took its design cues from the smaller AJS 7R, including the engine case and covers painted gold.

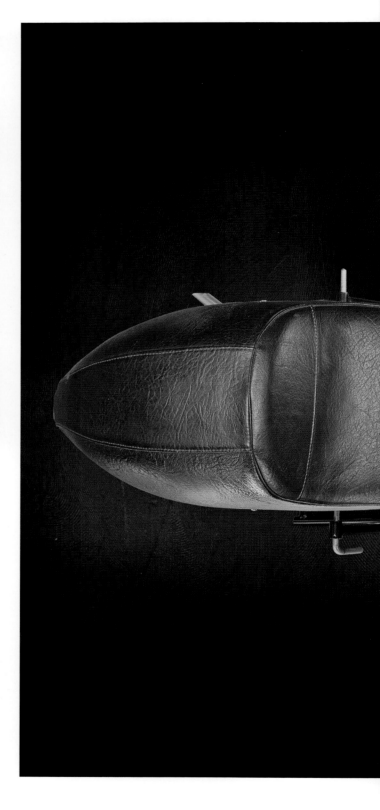

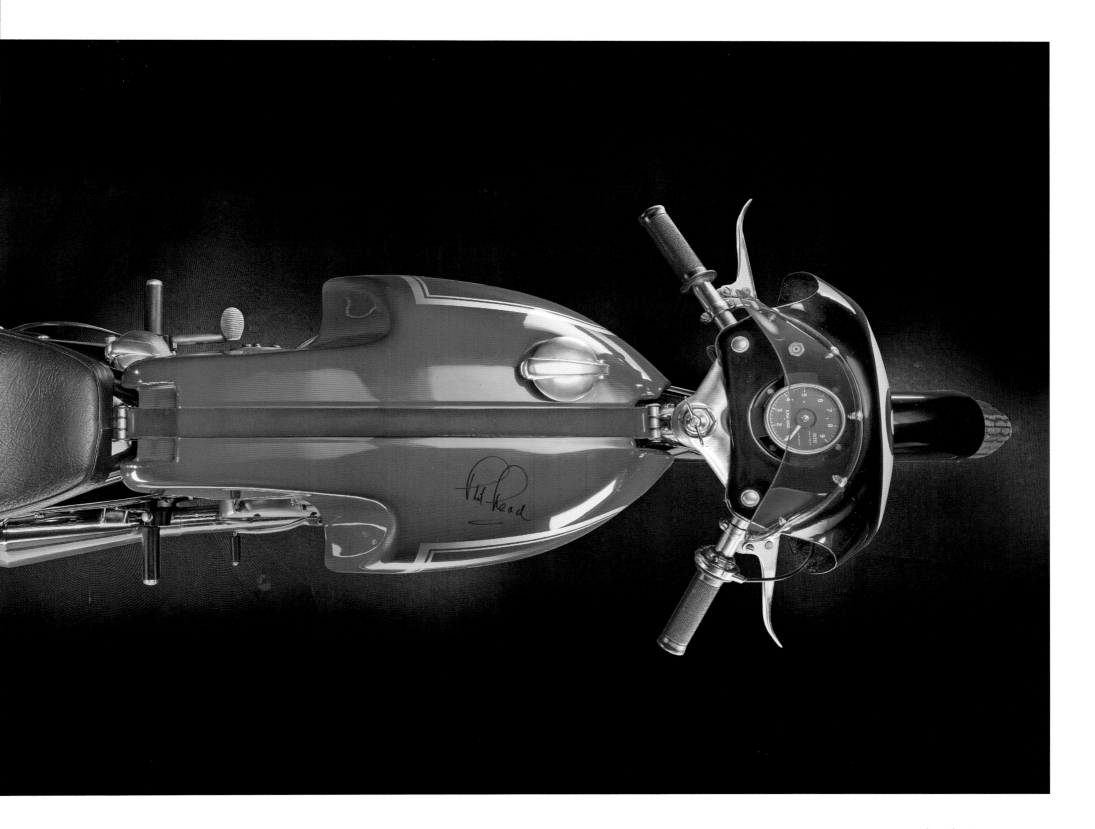

CHAPTER 18

1936 Zündapp K800

The German company that became Zündapp, a partnership among the Krupp and Thiel companies, was originally an armaments manufacturer in Nuremberg, providing weapons and other implements of destruction through World War I. When business understandably declined after the war, entrepreneur Fritz Neumeyer coalesced the Nuremberg firm into the Zunder und Apparatebau ("igniter and apparatus") company. Enthusiasts quickly discarded the name in favor of the simpler moniker Zündapp. Neumeyer took over as sole proprietor and embarked on a long journey building scooters, motorcycles, and cars for everyday Germans.

The first Zündapp motorcycle was the Z22 in 1921. Neumeyer named it Motorrad für Jedermann ("motorcycle for everyone"). This was an early iteration of a developing German ethos of equality and prosperity that grew, with some help from Zündapp, into the Volkswagen ("people's car") legacy. At any rate, the early Zündapps were intended it to be simple, reliable bikes—two-stroke singles and twins to move people around the cities and the country.

In the 1930s, Zündapp started building bigger, heavier four strokes—the K series—with more power to compete with BMW, DKW, and other European favorites. The bikes ranged in size from 200cc to 800cc and predictably used a shaft drive system that was enclosed in a crankcase, while also using the less predictable stamped-steel frame, an idea that may possibly have been borrowed from Neander. The K bikes put Zündapp on the world stage, quickly

building the company's market share and popularity before the World War II. By the time the company folded in the early 1980s, Zündapp had produced nearly three million motorcycles.

The K bikes were the crown jewel of Zündapp. The smaller 500 and 600cc runners were flat twins in the same style as competitor BMWs. These bikes, particularly the KS600, were often paired with sidecars and produced in great numbers for the Wehrmacht. The KS750, a heavier and more reliable wartime model, featured a driven third wheel and replaced the KS600 as the preferred tool of German soldiers and officers. These bikes were so well designed that many remain on the road today, cared for and ridden by Zündapp aficionados. After the war, Zündapp discontinued the 750 and went back to an improved version of the 600 twin, releasing it anew as the KS601, an astonishingly heavy but reliable motorcycle also known as the "green elephant."

Stunning to look at and a thrill to ride, the K800 was a bike that was, in some ways, forty years ahead of its time. First introduced in 1933, the bike used a unit construction design around a horizontally opposed, 800cc four-stroke in a flat-four configuration with shaft drive—an idea that didn't return to motorcycling until Honda created the Gold Wing. The K800 was the only four-cylinder

The Zündapp employed front and rear brakes but no rear suspension. And while the bike may look massive, it only weighed about 450 pounds with its tank full.

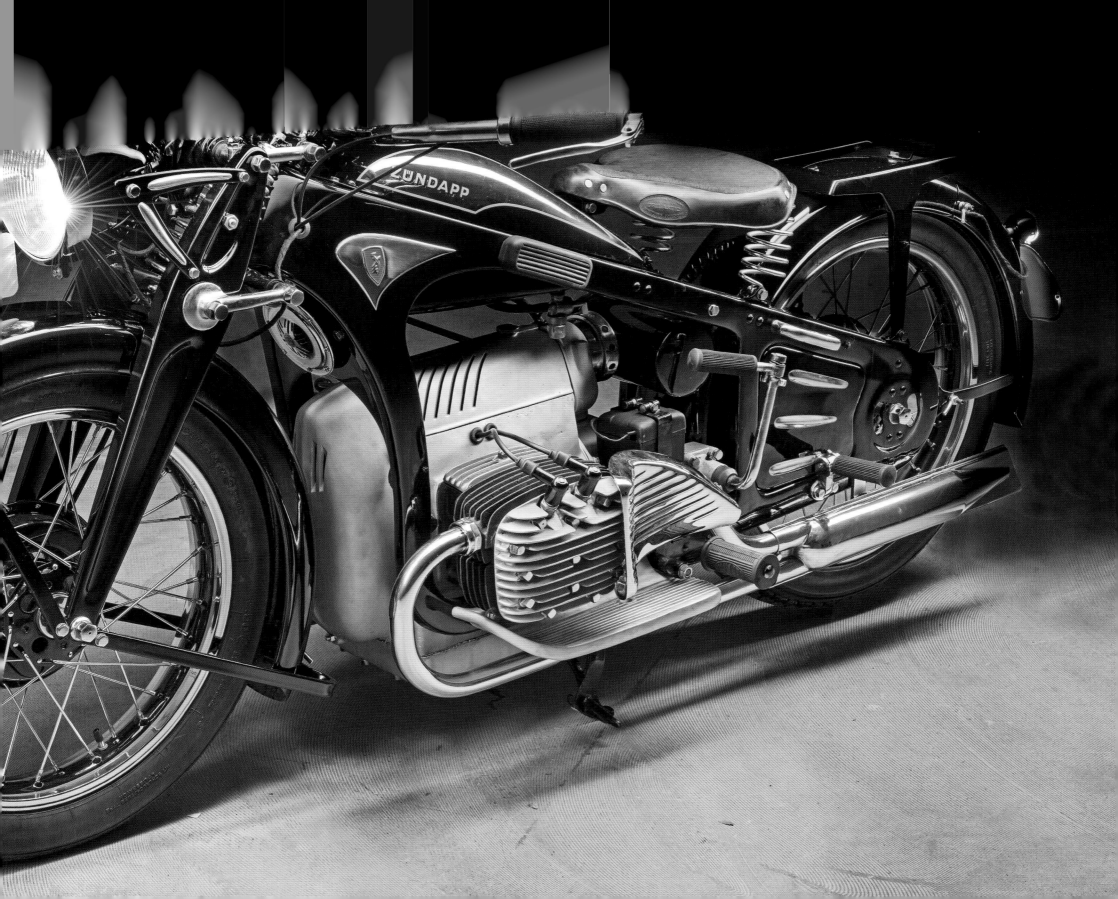

motorcycle used by the German military during World War II.

After the war, the company buckled down to get Germany moving again and started building many smaller two-stroke single and twin machines, and more notably the Bella scooter. Zündapp was also known for building the iconic microcars that became familiar and useful throughout Europe and the developing world. The company made good use of its resources over time and churned out hundreds of thousands of bikes, but eventually lost market share and profitability during the cold war. The company folded in 1984.

Right: Due to the large number of these bikes still intact around the world, Zündapps can be bought for a fraction of the price of other classic marques and are great fun to ride, wrench, and show off.

Opposite page: Twisting the throttle grip of the 1936 Zündapp K800 guns the 800cc, opposed four with shaft-drive, encased within the unmistakable Zundapp pressed-steel frame.

1936 ZÜNDAPP K800 SPECIFICATIONS:

Engine type:
Air-cooled, boxer or horizontally opposed four

Displacement:
804 cubic centimeters

Horsepower:
22

Special feature:
Only 4-cylinder motorcycle used by the German military in World War II.

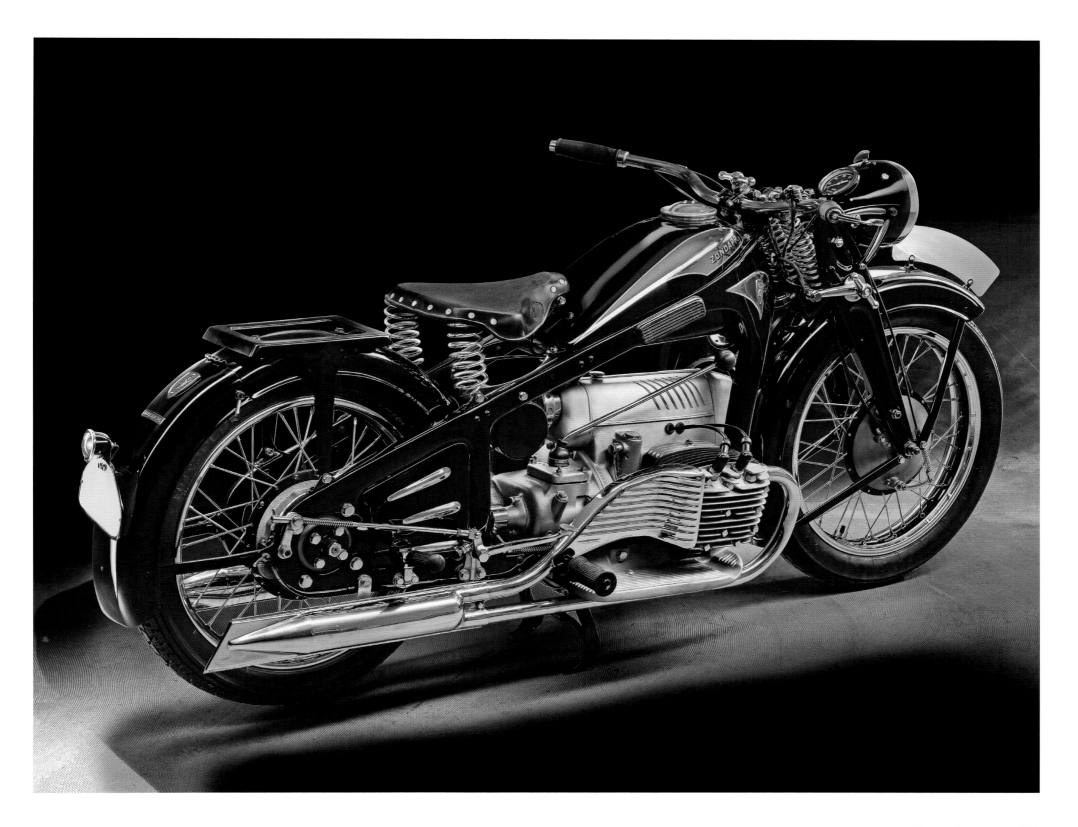

1938 Benelli Monotubo

Benelli began life in Pesaro, Italy, in 1911 as a repair and fabrication shop run by six brothers: Antonio, Domenico, Filippo, Francesco, Giuseppe, and Giovanni Benelli. The firm started producing small, lightweight single-cylinder motorcycles in the early 1920s. Early track prowess (the youngest brother Antonio was a gifted racer) propelled Benelli to compete with the big dogs, such as DKW, Excelsior, and Rudge. Riding a specially produced 175 meant only for the track, "Tonino" won the Italian championship in 1927, 1928, 1930, and 1931. These weekend demonstrations of Benelli power and style led to a healthy share of customers in the street motorcycle market.

Tonino's racing career unfortunately ended early, with a devastating crash in 1932. Benellis ridden by Italians won the European Championships in 1932 and 1934, and Ted Mellors later took a Benelli 250 to win the Lightweight Isle of Man TT race in 1939. By this time, the company was confident in its bikes' racing prospects and set to debut its supercharged version the following year. The war intervened,

and Benelli limited its competition to the Italian championship. World War II took a heavy toll on the factory, so it was forced to sell unused military bikes to the public until production resumed years later.

By 1950, Benelli was manufacturing zillions of small singles, popular the world over as simple, inexpensive transportation. The group didn't delve into twins and multis until the 1970s, when it was acquired by new owner Alejandro de Tomaso, who merged Benelli with Moto Guzzi, in an attempt to compete with the incoming waves of Japanese motorcycles. The shining star of this effort was the Benelli Sei, a breathtaking 750cc inline six, but it was not meant to be. Plagued by "personality," the production of traditional Benelli bikes' ended in the late 1980s. After some fits and starts, though, limited production of Benelli motorcycles has resumed. Currently, various models of 300–1,100cc sporting twins, triples, and fours are exported mostly to India, making Benelli the oldest Italian and European bike manufacturer still functioning today.

The 250cc single put out 27 horsepower at 9,500 rpm, enough to reach over 110 miles per hour—capable of running head-to-head with its competitor, the Guzzi single.

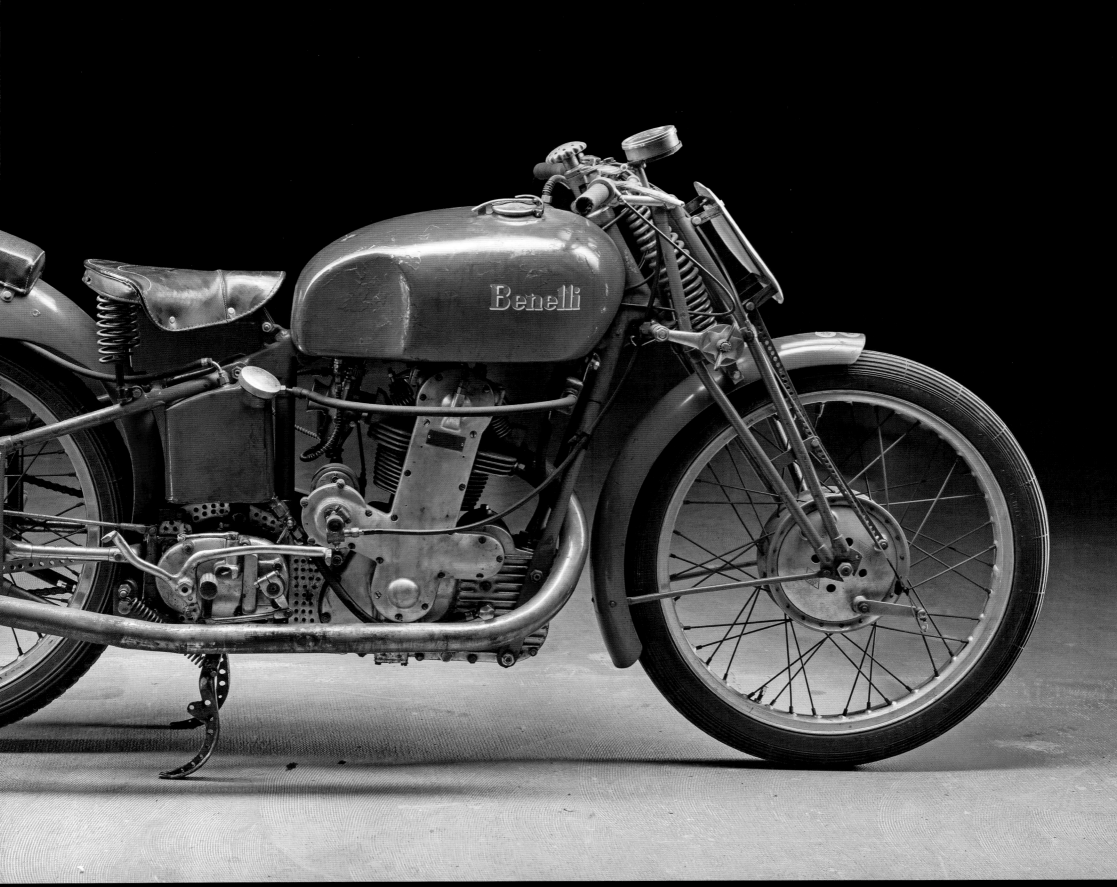

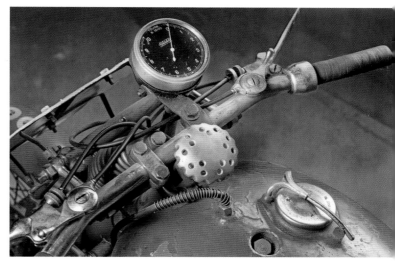

A bike built for speed on the racetrack doesn't need fancy gadgets and gauges at the dash. A straight-up tachometer showing 10,000+ rpms was all a rider needed.

Above: The 1938 250cc Benelli used friction-damped girder forks and a rear swingarm, plus the huge alloy brakes needed to slow the bike at breakneck speeds.

Opposite page: The Benelli brothers, ever mindful of ways to gain an advantage on the racetrack, turned in the late 1930s to supercharged singles and multi-cylinder racebikes.

1938 BENELLI 250–A BARNFIND–
SPECIFICATIONS:

Engine type:
Air-cooled, supercharged DOHC single

Displacement:
250 cubic centimeters

Horsepower:
27

Special feature:
This model won an Isle of Man TT race
in 1939. A sophisticated hand-built
double overhead camshaft race engine
complete with supercharger.

CHAPTER 20

1938 DKW ss350

Ith its 125cc single and 350cc twin two-strokes that appeared in the 1930s, DKW is responsible for some of the most numerous and popular bikes in the world. The moniker DKW might come from a steam-engined automobile called the Dampf Kraft Wagen ("steam driven car"); it might be a more pedestrian reference to its famous 125cc engine, known as "das kleine wunder" (small wonder or little marvel). Either way, the original company, Zschopauer Maschinenfabrik, founded in 1906 in Zchopau, Germany, started life as a builder of machines for the textile industry. In 1919 DKW began producing a small, two-stroke engine that sold very well after World War I. In fact, the engine was a perfect match when fitted to the bicycles of the day, so the company started producing bicycles in the early 1920s, then purpose-built 150cc motorized bicycles, precursors of modern scooter designs with large floorboards and the engine under the rider's seat. Soon after, motorcycle production followed.

While many of its competitors were offering large, heavy, complex four-stroke machines, DKW was able to wring 15 horsepower out of a simple, 125cc two-stroke engine with really only four moving parts. The design's simplicity made the bikes inexpensive to produce and sell; their reliability made them useful and popular. DKW quickly became one of the biggest European manufacturers, building singles, twins, and triples from 100cc to 1,000cc for hundreds of thousands of motorcycles and automobiles until the Great Depression.

To survive the Depression, DKW joined forces with Audi, Horch, and Wanderer to form the Auto Union, its marque represented by four interlocking circles that is still recognizable in the Audi emblem today. The RT 125, designed by Hermann Weber, is widely accepted as the motorcycle that inspired numerous other manufacturers, including BSA, Harley-Davidson, Honda, and Yamaha. DKW racers won the European championship four times before World War II, as well as competing successfully in the Isle of Man TT and International Six Days Trials in the 1930s, demonstrating not only simple and effective motorcycle design but reliable power and road-holding suspension.

In addition to being successful with the public, the German army used the smaller DKW bikes in addition to the bigger, heavier BMWs and Zündapps, and relied on DKW's lightweight 125cc and 350cc bikes for dispatch duty during World War II. DKW assembly shifted to West Germany after the war, and modest production resumed. The company tried to build a few mopeds, but the designs never became popular. By 1960 DKW had disappeared into the grouping of Daimler-Benz and the Zweirad Union, and not long after, production of all the bikes under its badge had stopped.

But the story doesn't end there. In the east, production was flourishing. As a war spoil, the

The bike shown is an SS350 factory racing bike that was never sold to the public.

The water-cooled DKW SS350 used a supercharging piston along with a rare (but not unheard-of) two-pistons-per-cylinder design, effectively making this two-stroke twin a five-cylinder bike.

Opposite page: A split-twin, 250cc supercharged racer similar to this DKW SS350 set a speed record of 114 miles per hour in 1938 and won the 1938 Isle of Man TT junior class.

The little 350cc twin, with a girder fork, plunger rear suspension, and pressed steel frame, made extensive use of magnesium components and cranked out nearly 35 horsepower.

DKW machinery was stripped from Germany by the occupying Soviets and moved. Designs and tooling appropriated, production of the popular NZ 350 resumed in Russia. Understanding there is little need to mess with a good thing, the Soviets cleverly branded their bike the IZH 350. (A version of the RT 125, copied and produced after the war, was still in production in the twenty-first century in Minsk.)

The legalized bootlegging of DKW bike designs didn't stop there. Another notable resurrection of DKW motorcycles was that of Motorrad Zschopau (MZ). After the war, the original factory started producing the RT and NZ bikes again, and not long after developed a line of 125–250cc engines to use with MZ scooters. The British company BSA got hold of the RT 125 design after the war, and in 1948 released the Bantam, which became one of the best-selling British bikes of all time. Harley-Davidson also built the RT 125 for a dozen years after the war, badged at first as the Model 125, then later as the Hummer. Ariel, a BSA subsidiary, also received designs for the DKW parallel twin, but the funky and futuristic Leader into which they installed it was a flop. And the RT and NZ two-stroke designs can still be found today in millions of simple, reliable Japanese bikes largely unknown to the western world.

1938 DKW SS350 REPLICA SPECIFICATIONS:

Engine type:
Water-cooled, 2-stroke, 4-piston twin with supercharger

Displacement:
350 cubic centimeters

Horsepower:
34

Special feature:
Unique "5-cylinder" engine comprised of two 2-piston cylinders and a fifth-piston supercharger.

CHAPTER 21

1939 BMW Rennsport Kompressor

Germany's Gottlieb Daimler invented the world's first motorcycle in 1885, a clever wooden contraption with sophisticated linkages and a twist-grip brake, but the Daimler name is better known for the four-wheeled vehicles that became his obsession. The true enthusiasm for motorcycles in Germany came much later, after World War I, from the likes of Neckarsulm Strickmaschinen Union (NSU), Dampf-Kraft-Wagen (DKW), and Bayerische Motoren Werke (BMW).

When you think of BMW, think of endlessly spinning wheels, driven by endlessly spinning flat twins with endlessly spinning driveshafts, soaking up the road. More than a few aircraft pilots have suggested that motorcycling is next best thing to flying—think of a BMW as an earthbound aircraft. These bikes float along, soaking in mile after mile of rural countryside, its riders seemingly without a care in the world.

And when you think of BMW, think also of Max Friz. Max Friz was a not only an engineer specializing in engine design, he was key to the founding of BMW. Friz worked for BMW from 1916 until 1945, primarily as chief designer and engineer for the company. He designed Germany's first useful and practicable aircraft engines in 1912 for Daimler before joining BMW. The engines had discrete cylinders jutting from

Georg Meier's win of the 1939 Isle of Man TT on a BMW 255 *Kompressor* was the first victory by a non-English racer in the prestigious Senior (500cc) class.

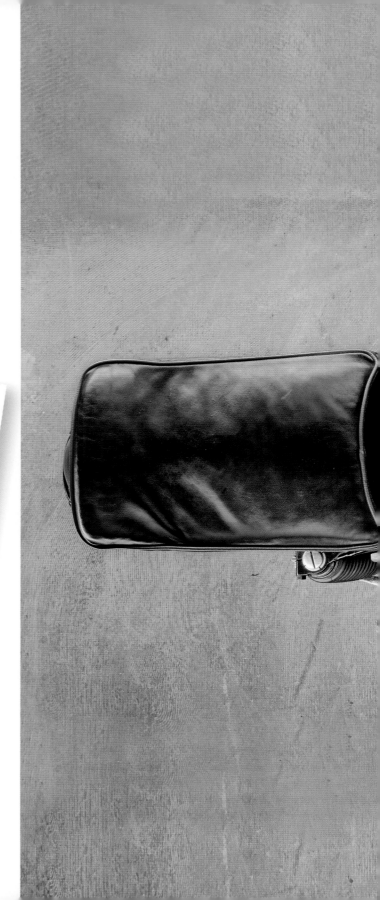

the crankcase and an overhead cam design, driven by a shaft and gears.

During World War I, Friz designed engines for the Reichswehr and achieved great success in keeping his company front and center when competing with Benz for war contracts. After the war, the Allies placed severe restrictions on Germany's manufacturing industry, so BMW, known previously for aircraft engines, switched to building motorcycles. Friz took his ideas for aircraft engines and put them to use in the company's first two-wheeler, creating in a few elegant strokes the concept of the "earthbound aircraft." After a short run producing engines for other motorcycle builders, in 1923 BMW unveiled the shaft-driven R32, with a 500cc powerplant. The engine's cylinders project from either side of the motorcycle out into the open air, a configuration that allows for reliable power and efficient cooling. This simple design led to better and better bikes that served the military and the public very well. In fact, this basic design came to represent the shape and sound of traditional BMW engines for the next one hundred years. A legend was born.

The BMW logo, also called "the roundel," was created shortly after World War I. To anyone who's ever seen an airplane and has the slightest bit of imagination, the logo is immediately recognizable as a spinning propeller against a cobalt-blue sky—a tribute to BMW's aviation manufacturing past.

BMW's first successes at competition came in the form of speed records set by native son Ernst Henne. Using a supercharged 750cc boxer, Henne set the record at 174 miles per hour in the 1930s that remained intact through 1950. In an intentional show of German strength, supercharged 500cc BMWs won the 1938 European Championship and the 1939 Isle of Man TT Senior class. Georg Meier, winner of the TT, hid his bike in a haystack during the war, only to retrieve it after the Berlin Wall fell, using it for a parade lap around the island.

After the war, supercharging in the world championship was banned, and so BMW gave up its attack on the world's podiums. The boxer remained a winner, however, in sidecar racing. Klaus Enders and Ralf Englehardt helped the BMW name take eighteen of twenty titles from 1955 to 1974, a winning run not equaled even by MV Agusta in two-wheeled competition.

BMW has a well-established reputation for stable, reliable twins that make great touring bikes. They also built singles right up until the 1960s, and again (with some success) starting in the 1990s, but their history is tied to the two-cylinder, air-cooled twin. With a consistently clean fit and finish, the company has successfully hitched its wagon to a traditional style and flat-twin boxer engine. With this design, BMW devised a winning combination of a simple and reliable flat twin and built chassis systems that allowed the bikes to handle any curve in Europe.

Until recently, BMW products have always fallen on the expensive side of the motorcycle spectrum, and for a long while they were relatively uncommon in the traffic mix. This exclusivity is not really a negative trait, because the bikes are also long-lived. (Boxer fans joke that the engine needs at least 100,000 miles on the clock before it's properly broken in.) This has helped create a worldwide network of devoted enthusiasts who speak with their wallets.

Today, BMW motorcycles are everywhere. And while they're not cheap, no longer are they the only expensive bikes in town. American bikes and big touring cruisers fetch premium prices too, helping the German bikes compete and earn a respectable market share among riders who favor curves and adventure over straight-line highway touring.

By the late 1930s, BMW had introduced a coil-spring plunger at the rear with a friction damper to keep the bouncing of the rear wheel under control.

Right: The clever use of magnesium for the engine casings and wheel hubs was complemented by a light weight, lugless frame built from lightweight but very strong tapered tubing.

The 1939 Rennsport used a modest 492cc boxer twin, supercharged, with dual-overhead cams. The cylinders were made from aluminum and the engine block from magnesium.

Above: BMW was quick to experiment with forced induction, bolting its first supercharger (*compressor*) to its overhead-valve racing machines as early as 1925.

Left: In Grand Prix racing during the 1930s, European manufacturers duked it out on newly built, high-speed racetracks. BMW and others upped the stakes with supercharged multis.

1938 BMW TYPE 255 RS500
SPECIFICATIONS:

Engine type:
Air-cooled, boxer or horizontally opposed,
DOHC twin cylinder with supercharger

Displacement:
492cc

Horsepower:
60

Special feature:
Aluminum cylinders with magnesium
crankcase and supercharger casing,
plunger rear suspension.

CHAPTER 22

1939 Vincent Series A Rapide, 1947 Series B Rapide, and 1949 Black Lightning

Vincent-HRD, makers of the "world's fastest motorcycles," started life in Stevenage, England, in 1928 when Philip Vincent purchased HRD Motors. At first, the bikes used brought-in engines from JAP and other companies, but by 1934 the company was producing the Meteor and Comet, which featured the company's own 500cc single. The spark that ignited the Vincent flame was designer Phil Irving, one of the more underrated names in motorcycle history. Beautiful and fast, Irving's bikes were popular, but expensive, which kept production relatively limited. In 1936, the company introduced the Rapide Series A, a 1,000cc twin that was, at the time, the fastest production bike in Europe.

The Series B Rapide followed after the war, featuring a better unit construction design in which the engine became a stressed member, replacing part of the frame. The Rapides were also notable for their four-drum braking system—attentive concern for

stopping almost was a new phenomenon in the 1940s. The Series C followed soon after, improving the already excellent suspension and handling with the new Girdraulic fork, a girder fork with hydraulic damping.

The Vincent motorcycles stand out in history as being some of the most stunning bikes ever built, and the Black Shadow was the company's halo machine. Irving's masterpiece, the fire-breathing, 1,000cc Black Shadow, was the fastest stock motorcycle on the planet—a title it held for twenty-four years, from 1949 to 1972. The Black Shadow stands out as being one of the most beautiful motorcycles in existence: a Ducati 916 without the muscle shirt. Seen from the starboard side, the cylinders, intakes, and exhausts look decidedly like a living, breathing human

The 1939 Series A Rapide used a cantilever rear suspension (which was adapted to later models), a foot gear-change, four-speed gearbox, and kickstand.

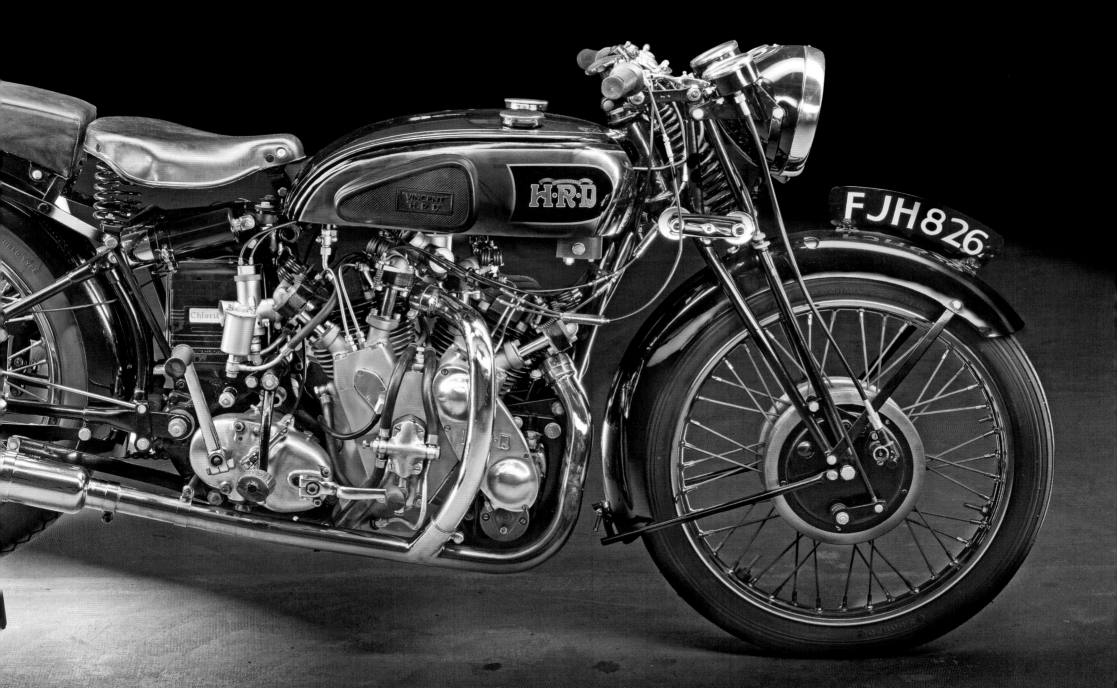

heart—even the case cover was heart-shaped. Like the Brough Superior, the Black Shadow was built for power and speed, but came at a price few could afford in the day.

Designed by Phil Irving, the Black Shadow was the genius juxtaposition of postwar humility (steel building materials were in short supply) and economy of design. The engine, made from aluminum alloy, became a stressed member. A triangle-shaped swinging arm, very similar to mono-shock designs not common until the 1970s, was bolted directly to the engine—the overall design not dissimilar to the Britten V1000. With a short wheelbase, this bike was the ultimate combination of power and handling. It was on a tuned Black Shadow that Rollie Free stripped down to bathing trunks in 1948 and set the record for a non-supercharged bike at Bonneville, the first to break the 150-mile-per-hour barrier.

Hunter S. Thompson was a raving fan of the Black Shadow, citing its influence on him in *Fear and Loathing in Las Vegas* and other works. The level of detail and love that went into the building of Vincent machines is obvious, but they were twice the price of their competitors' models, which helped ensure the company was out of business by the mid-1950s. Love like that wasn't sustainable in a market reliant on mass production. Production of these unforgettable motorcycles ceased in 1955.

The Vincent motorcycles—including this 1939 Rapide—were truly stunning. Their fluid shape and symmetry made them appear almost like living things.

1939 VINCENT RAPIDE SERIES A SPECIFICATIONS:

Engine type:
Air-cooled, OHV V-twin

Displacement:
998 cubic centimeters

Horsepower:
45

Special feature:
Early 47.5-degree motor preceded the more-familiar 50 degree of the later B- and C-series.

When first introduced in 1939, the Vincent Rapide Series A was the fastest production bike on the European continent, thanks to Phil Irving's 1,000cc design.

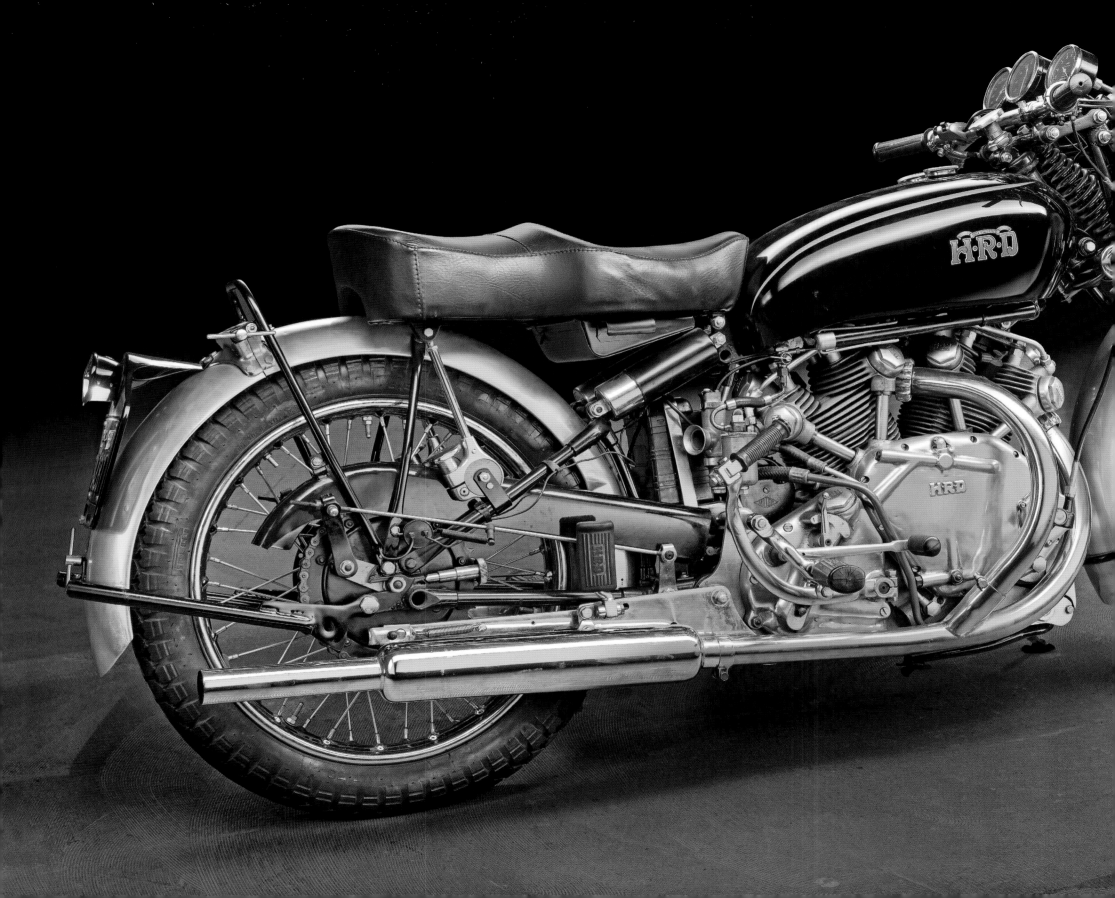

Fewer than two thousand Series B Rapides were ever produced, which only adds to the long-running drama, mystery, and pride in owning a Vincent twin.

Left: Series B wheels were detachable. The rear wheel was also reversible and could be fitted with different sprockets for quick gear-ratio changes.

1947 VINCENT RAPIDE SERIES B SPECIFICATIONS:

Engine type:
Air-cooled, OHV V-twin

Displacement:
998 cubic centimeters

Horsepower:
45

Special feature:
Large headlamp, friction-damped girder front forks, 50-degree V-twin with improved gearbox.

Vincent's 1,000cc V-twin offered both refinement and tremendous (for the period) performance.

US comedian and motorcycle enthusiast Jay Leno was astonished by the Vincent's ride and once quipped that the cylinders fired about "once every lamppost."

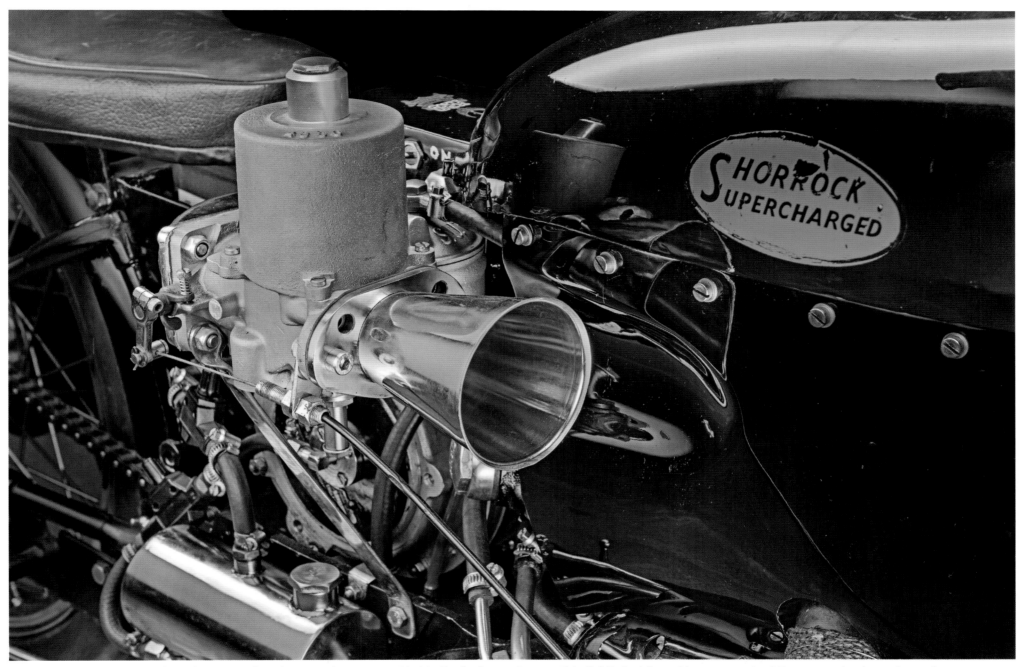

The Black Lighting was built for ultimate speed, and a supercharger was added in the (quite nearly correct) belief that adding a blower guaranteed the owner a land-speed record.

Left: Stock, the Black Lightning came from the factory competition-ready, with roadrace tires, lightweight aluminum wheels and fenders, magnesium alloy engine components, rearsets, and a solo seat.

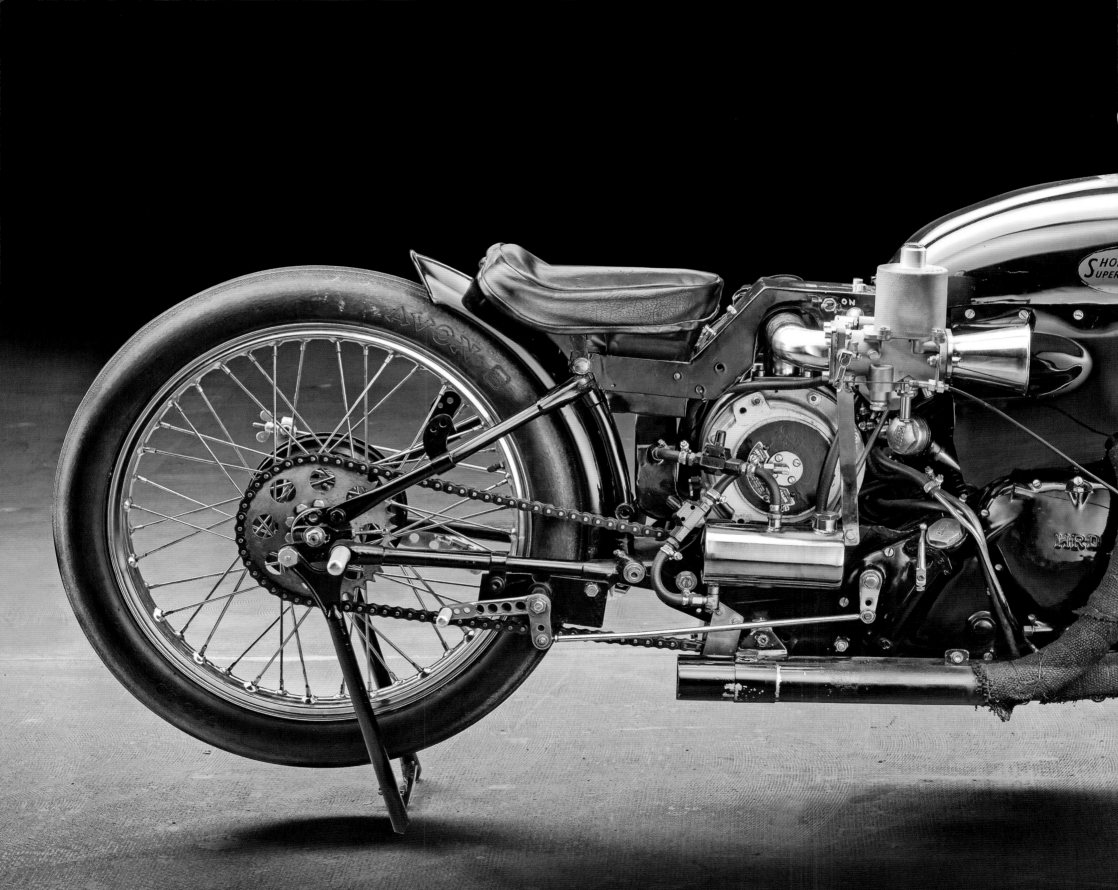

Only thirty 1949 Vincent Black Lightnings were officially ever made. This one was lengthened by several inches and supercharged to improve chances of breaking speed records.

1949 VINCENT BLACK LIGHTNING SPECIFICATIONS:

Engine type:
Air-cooled, OHV V-twin with Shorrock supercharger

Displacement:
998 cubic centimeters

Horsepower:
72 (stock)

Special feature:
The Joe Simpson bike that was modified for his speed record attempts and was also ridden by Vincent stalwart Marty Dickerson.

CHAPTER 23

1940 Crocker

The Crocker motorcycle was a short-lived, but memorable, phenomenon in southern California during the 1930s. The company was known for making powerful racing singles, twins, and even scooters until its trajectory changed in 1942 and the company refocused on crafting aircraft parts.

Albert Crocker was a designer and engineer for both the Aurora and Indian manufacturing companies in the American Midwest before World War II. He learned the ropes on some of the finest high-performance twins in the country, including the legendary "White Thors," then packed up and moved to Denver, Colorado, while working for Indian, and then Kansas City, Missouri, to operate his own Indian dealership. But the West Coast was calling to him; he sold out and moved to Venice (Los Angeles), buying another dealership and, on the side, building his own bikes.

For the first few years of production, Crocker built fast, reliable racing singles known as the Small Tanks. These were purpose-built race bikes, designed to beat the most powerful contenders in the world, and they made the Crocker name renown on racetracks. These tiny bikes with chrome-moly frames cranked out more than 40 horsepower from their 500cc engines, making them the fastest things on the speedways in the United States, knocking their Harley-Davidson and Indian competitors for a loop. All the best racers on the West Coast speedway circuits and most of the podium finishes at the time went to riders on Crockers.

The first Crocker 45-degree V-twins, also known as "Big Tanks," appeared with 1,000cc engines with an advanced cylinder head design that put 50–60 horsepower to the rear wheel—half again as much as its US contemporaries and giving it an easy 90-mile-per-hour cruising speed. (In a show of pure sportsmanship, Crocker later developed an aftermarket head kit for Indian twins, which increased their horsepower significantly.) As customers' need for power and speed got stronger, boring the cylinders and increasing the size of the pistons led to engine sizes up to 1,500cc, the biggest displacement on the continent at the time. These bikes were built meticulously by hand, with parts made in the Crocker machine shop. These machines could be considered the ancestors of postwar custom bikes, and even the superbikes of later years.

The Crocker twins were legendary at the time for their beauty, performance, and speed. It's been said that the Big Tank's design is "so perfect, the bike seems to be moving even when standing still." Crocker custom built each bike specifically for its waiting customer, who could choose the color, adornments, trim, and even the transmission's gear ratios. But Crocker's focus over all else was speed—he wanted his bikes to be the fastest on the road and on the speedway. The company sold bikes with a

Few Crocker bikes (let alone Big Tanks like this 1940 model) were ever produced—only about one hundred in all, pushing prices to $250,000 at auction today.

guarantee of sorts: owners were welcome to a full refund of their purchase price if the bike was ever outrun by a stock Harley-Davidson or Indian of the same displacement. It was reported in that no refund was ever given.

Only about one hundred Crocker twins were ever built, a boutique's boutique bike, and the machines can fetch $250,000–275,000 at auction today. Where the English Brough Superior was known as the Rolls-Royce of motorcycles, the Crocker was known as the Duesenberg. Unfortunately, when World War II hit and the world diverted focus and resources to the war effort, Crocker became another casualty of the times and quit the business. Because of the exclusivity of these bikes and the romance surrounding California motorcycle culture, rumors abound about Crocker motorcycles and their manufacture, use as police bikes, quarrels with Harley-Davidson—great drama and intrigue surely helpful in driving up the price of a barn find.

Recently, an enthusiast fabricator of motorcycle parts has acquired the rights to the Crocker name and begun producing, in very small quantities, high-quality replicas of the esteemed bikes for wealthy customers. The new Big- and Small-Tank Crockers cost about $150,000—a nice discount from an original these days.

Ostensibly built for speed and speed alone, the Crocker's finish and attention to detail made them showpieces worthy of winning beauty contests, too.

The Crockers were said to have come with a guarantee from the factory: Your full purchase price would be refunded if beaten by a Harley or an Indian.

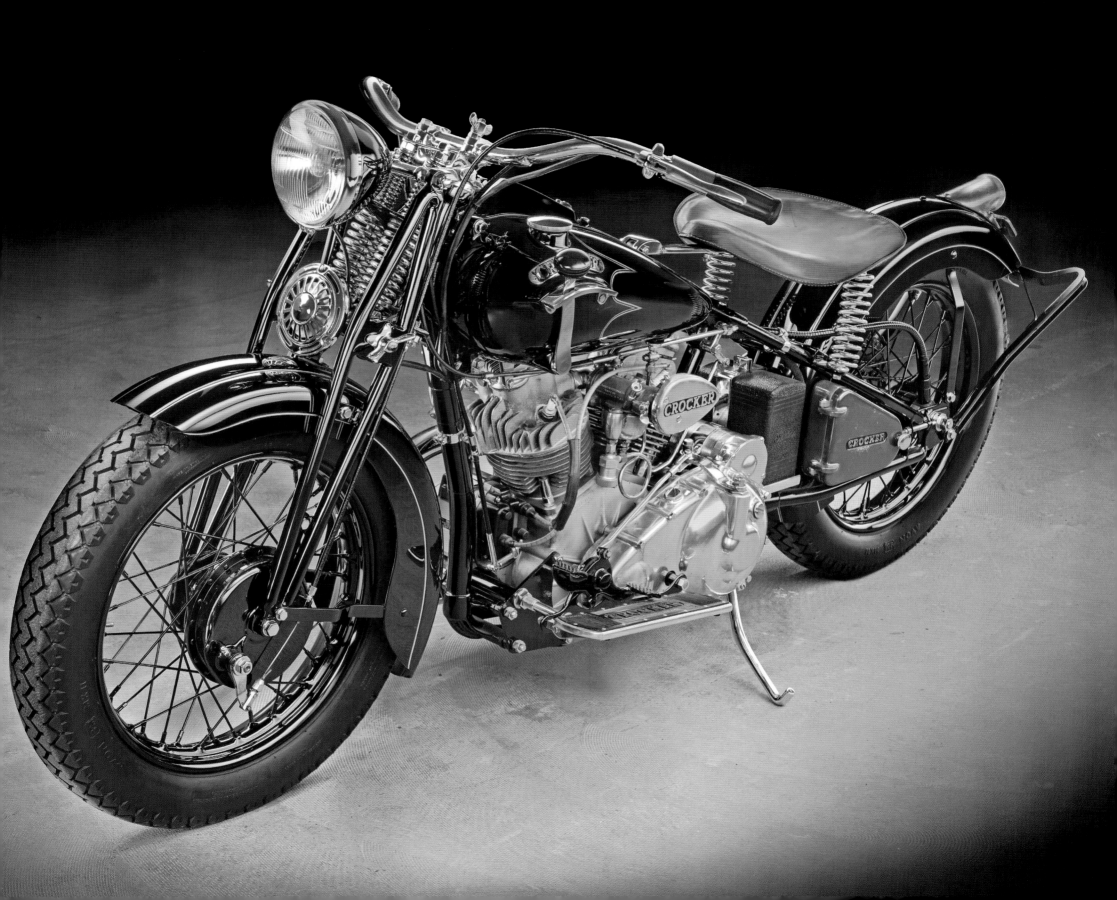

Crockers were built painstakingly, one at a time, with all parts made in the Crocker machine shop. The bike's intended buyer could choose color, trim, even gear ratios.

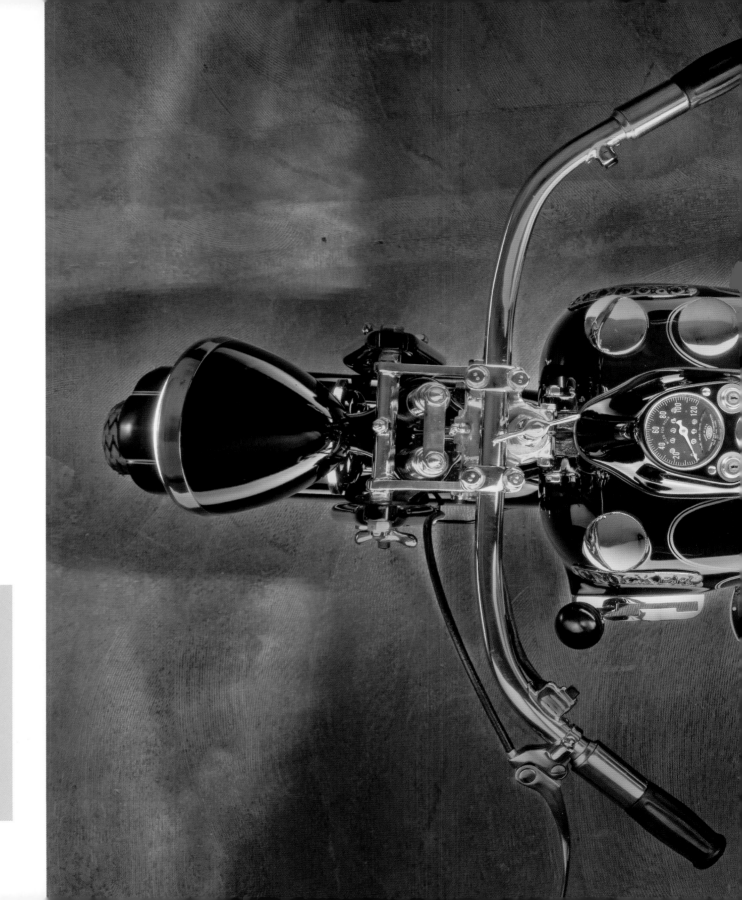

1940 CROCKER BIG TANK SPECIFICATIONS:

Engine type:
Air-cooled, OHV V-twin

Displacement:
1,491 cubic centimeters

Horsepower:
60

Special feature:
Fantastic attention to detail in every aspect, rare and fast in their day.

CHAPTER 24

1951 Velocette KTT Mark Eight and 1966 Thruxton

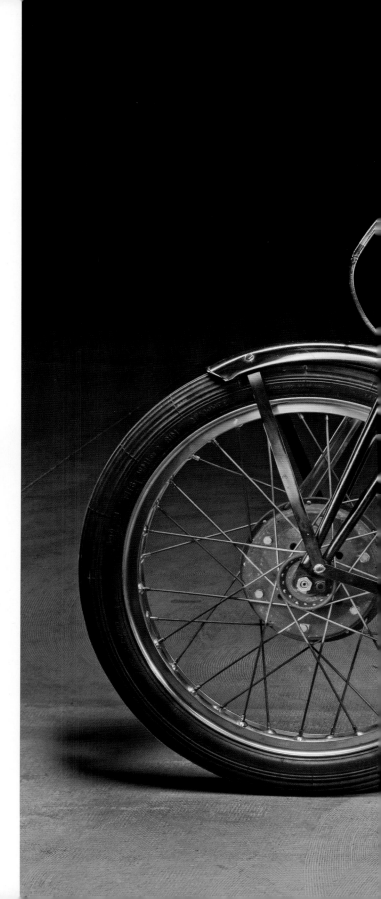

Another English manufacturer, the Veloce company was a small concern founded in Birmingham by a German-born Brit Johannes Gutgemann (later, John Goodman) in 1904. Joining the fray of motorcycle manufacturing on a small scale, the firm had its earliest success with 250cc two-stroke singles; the first were named Velocettes. These hand-built bikes were relatively advanced and unique for the time, with features such as throttle-controlled oil pumps and positive-stop foot shifters. Veloce, however, didn't show its hand until the 1920s, when its bikes started winning races.

The Velocettes grew into powerful, four-stroke singles of 350–500cc displacements. Race-ready bikes such as the KTT and KSS (350s) made the news and were favorites of private racers, while at the dealerships, sales of the 350cc MAC and 500cc MSS kept the money rolling in. Racing success after World War II helped Veloce continue its upward trend, resulting in the fabulous Venom and Viper singles of the 1950s, available to the public and set up for either street or racing.

An early Venom set a still-standing world record, averaging 100 miles per hour for a twenty-four

The Velocette KTT was a race-ready bruiser that could win on Sunday to help sell its tamer, milder brother, the MAC, on Monday in the dealerships.

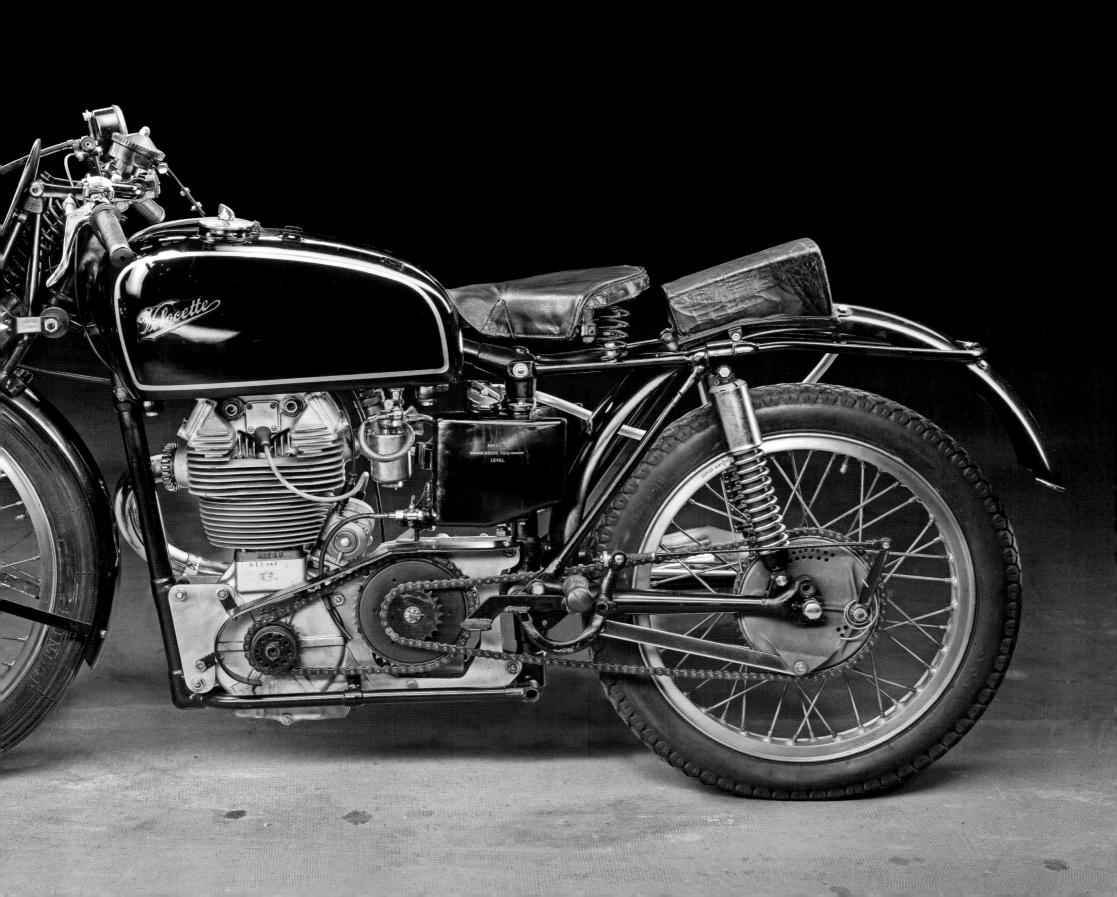

hour period—the first motorcycle of any size to do so. Then came the Venom Thruxton, a highly tuned single with alloy rims and twin leading shoe drum brakes churning out 40 horsepower, a favorite of street racers in the 1960s. It is remarkable that the Velocettes were able to compete at all in a market then dominated by the British twins from BSA, Norton, Triumph, and Vincent.

Unfortunately, the success of the Velocettes didn't change the fact that production numbers were small, the bikes were relatively expensive, and racing cost a small fortune. Worse, rather than keeping and improving its tradition of large capacity, racing singles, the firm diverted its focus and started building small-displacement LE model flat twins (nicknamed "noddie bikes") to attract buyers interested in cheap transportation. Rather than a runaway success, the new LE was a dead end that signaled the demise of the company.

One high note for the LE, though, was that it was popular for a time with police officers. Legend has it that UK patrol officers were required to salute superior officers while on duty. Once the cops started patrolling on Velocettes, taking their hand off the handlebars and straightening up into a respectful salute became risky, so officers were allowed to salute with smart nod—offering a possible explanation for the "noddies" nickname.

Even though the last of the Velocettes were well made, they were still too expensive and lacked popularity. There was a brief spark of life in the late 1960s, when Velocettes became popular desert, endure, and scramble racers in the United States, but survival was not to be. Shortly after the motorcycling world changed in 1969, Velocette sold off its assets and quit the motorcycle business.

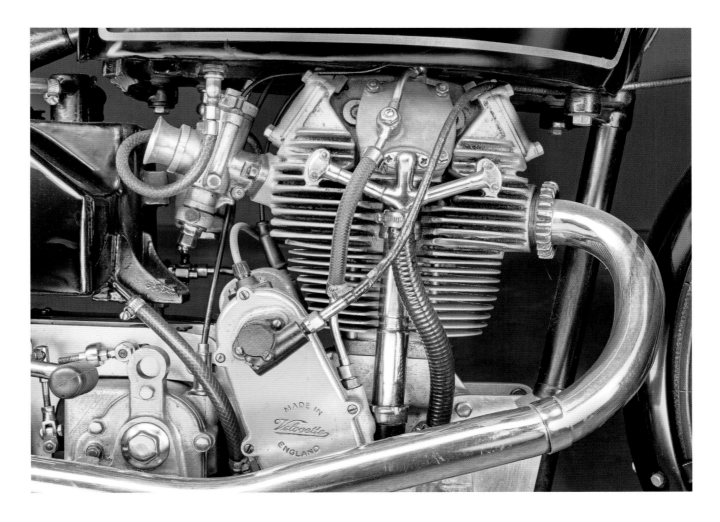

The KTT ran a 350cc, overhead-cam, air-cooled single good for 27 horsepower and capable of propelling the bike forward at 115 miles per hour.

The KTTs were blisteringly fast on the track. Both street and track models came with rearset pegs, alloy wheels, clip-on handlebars, and magnesium brake drums front and rear.

1951 VELOCETTE KTT MK 8
SPECIFICATIONS:

Engine type:
Air-cooled, SOHC single

Displacement:
348 cubic centimeters

Horsepower:
27

Special feature:
Along with the AJS 7R, this motorcycle dominated international Grand Prix racing until the Italian multicylinder motorcycles appeared on the scene.

Venom Thruxton buyers could get a tame street or race model with a high-performance cylinder head. Both came with rearsets, alloy wheels, clip-ons, and twin brake drums up front.

Opposite page: In 1967, Neil Kelly and Keith Heckles rode Thruxtons to first and second place in the 500cc Isle of Man TT production class. Champion Kelly recorded the fastest lap that year at 91 miles per hour.

Above: The "fishtail" mufflers were a stylistic feature of Velocette motorcycles since before World War II.

Opposite page: Drum brakes required cooling air to keep from overheating when used in competition.

1966 VELOCETTE VENOM THRUXTON
SPECIFICATIONS:

Engine type:
Air-cooled, OHV single

Displacement:
499 cubic centimeters

Horsepower:
40

Special feature:
A quality motorcycle, the Velocette single retained the "pre-war" fishtail muffler through to the company's demise

CHAPTER 25

1953 NSU Rennmax and 1955 Sport Max

ounded in southern Germany in 1873 and soon after headquartered in the town of Neckarsulm, NSU (Neckarsulm Strickmaschinen Union) was known originally as a factory that produced knitting machines. In the late 1800s, bicycles had become much more popular and profitable in Europe, so the company switched to bicycle production. The success of their bicycles and need for more speed compelled the founder Christian Schmidt to try his hand at motorized bicycles, and in 1901, the first NSU motorcycle was introduced bearing a Swiss-made engine.

Schmidt was not one to mess around with boutique machine production. By 1904 the company was producing its own engines and had a half dozen bike models lined up and ready for sale to the public, including one of the first European V-twins. They quickly ramped up displacement and production, and within five years had one of the largest bikes on the continent, a 1,000cc V-twin. In 1929, Norton's chief designer Walter Moore moved to NSU and created the company's first models featuring overhead cams, and many of the subsequent bikes looked, and sounded, suspiciously like Nortons. Of particular likeness was the SS, a 500cc overhead-cam single capable of more than 90 miles per hour in 1931—a great race bike that kept the Norton riders honest.

The Rennmax 250 was introduced in 1952. Legendary champion Werner Haas raced a bike like this to the podium in every race he entered in the early 1950s.

NSU made concerted efforts to market their products with racing and speed. Early machines made solid showings in roadracing (an NSU placed fifth in the inaugural Isle of Man TT in 1907) and distance-endurance events (such as the New York–to Los Angeles–cross-country run) from the turn of the century well into the 1930s. Later machines set world land-speed competition records. Civilian production slowed during World War II as the company focused on the military needs of the Wehrmacht, but resumed quickly again after the war.

Postwar Europe was hungry for commerce and positively starving for personal transportation, which helped NSU ramp up production to world-class levels. The company churned out as many as three hundred fifty thousand vehicles (mostly motorcycles, but also cars and bicycles) a year in the 1950s, putting them in the same category as DKW and Triumph at the time—one of the biggest manufacturers in the world. NSU really hit its stride when it introduced its simple 125cc Fox (similar in utility to DKW's mainstay the RT125) and more importantly, its 250cc Max, a quick, easy, reliable, and affordable motorcycle that created a platform for future innovation. The bikes had a pressed-steel frame and leading link forks, but with a new and unusual overhead-cam engine design known as "Ultramax." The design used long, enclosed (invisible) connecting rods with eccentric discs that turned the camshafts.

1953 NSU RENNMAX 250
SPECIFICATIONS:

Engine type:
Air-cooled, DOHC parallel twin

Displacement:
247 cubic centimeters

Horsepower:
31

Special feature:
Magnificent hand-beaten aluminum tank, seat, and bodywork over a pressed-steel frame and monoshock rear suspension.

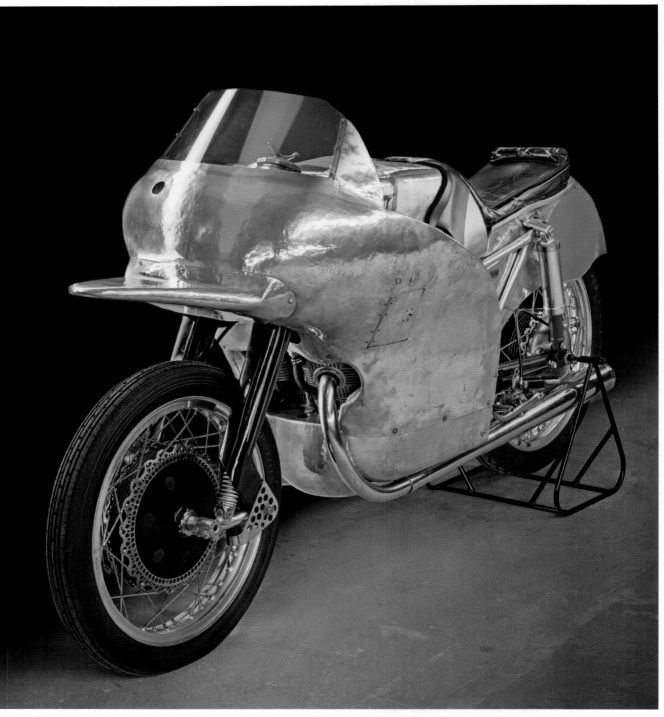

Set up for racing (and cooling), the rather ungainly front cowling cheated wind and allowed roadracers to push the bikes to 135 miles per hour.

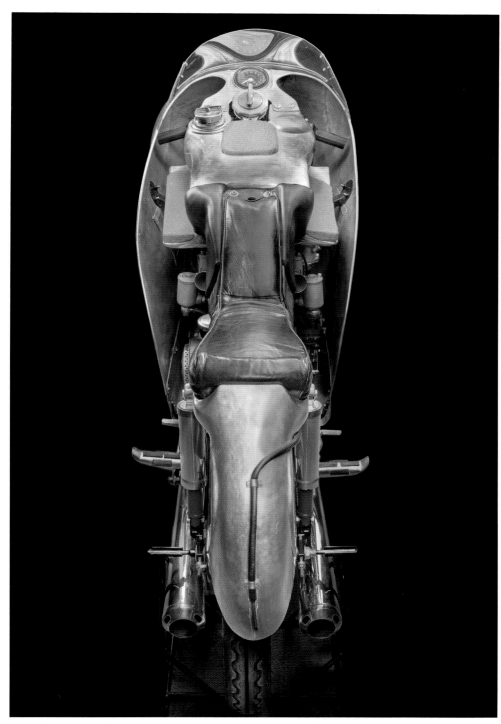

In 1956, a streamlined, supercharged version of the NSU Rennmax set a new world-speed record at the Bonneville Salt Flats with a recorded speed of 211 miles per hour.

Displacing 250cc, the four-stroke, air-cooled twin of the 1953 Rennmax 250 made nearly 40 horsepower at 11,500 rpm. The bike was slowed with sophisticated drum brakes front and rear.

New models sported monocoque frames of pressed steel and rear suspension, features that helped earn them notoriety and popularity. NSU motorcycles performed very well in top-speed competition during this time as well, earning its place in the world-record-speed books in 1951, 1953, 1954, and 1955. Another NSU amazed spectators by blasting down the German Autobahn during a timed attempt at a recorded 181 miles per hour on a supercharged 500cc race bike. In 1956, NSU descended on Bonneville, Utah, with a battery of six of its motorcycles of different sizes for the world land-speed record attempts, notably setting the new motorcycle record at 211 miles per hour with a streamlined, supercharged Rennsport.

The bikes of the day were the 50cc Quickly moped (which sold more than a million units between the years of 1953 and 1965), the 125cc Rennfox twin, the 250cc Sportmax single, and the 250cc Rennmax twin—a race version that won the world championship in 1953 and 1954. The Sportmax was a blistering-fast racer, an overhead-cam four stroke putting out close to 30 horsepower at 10,000 rpm with top speeds of more than 130 miles per hour. NSU quit racing after 1954 due to cost. Unfortunately, the higher-end Max bikes were more expensive to produce, making them less profitable and affordable in the 1950s. On the other side of the spectrum, the little Quickly was one of the world's most popular mopeds, filling the streets of Germany and neighboring countries at the rate of one thousand or more a day in the 1950s. Practically everybody had one of these. The two-stroke single engine was the perfect size, weight, and price in the European market.

All this success would not have come to an end, but NSU had for a long time diverted energy and focus to producing automobiles, which were much more profitable and in just as high demand in the late 1950s, and also in developing the Wankel rotary engine. By 1960, the company had lost its edge in the minds of consumers. The last Supermax emerged from the factory in 1963, and by 1965 NSU had quit the production of both motorcycles and mopeds. The failing company was bought up by Volkswagen and merged with Auto Union (Audi) and never returned to building bikes.

After overhead camshafts became common, wind resistance became racing motorcycles' greatest adversary. NSU race engineers took the challenge head-on.

To make up for the decision to drop works Grand Prix racing after 1954, NSU offered a racing version of their Max—the Sportmax—to privateers.

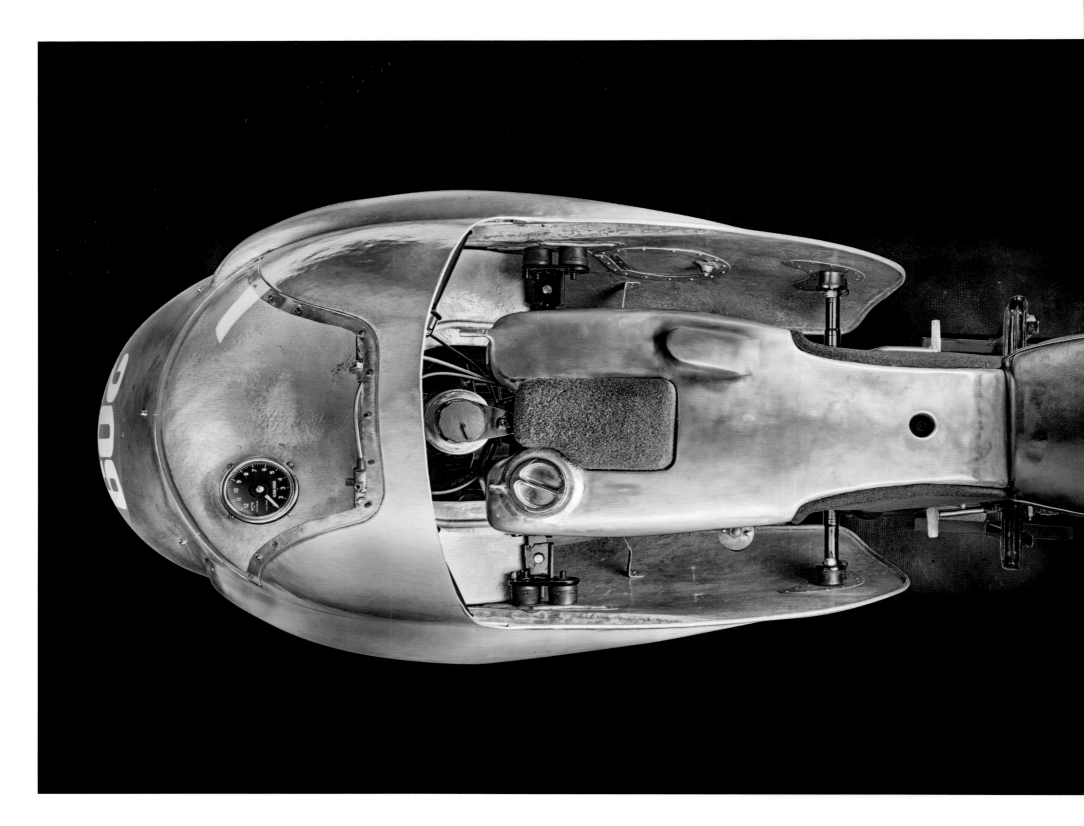

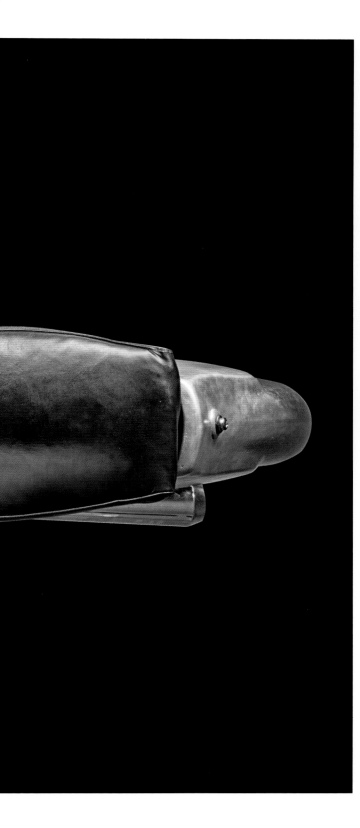

Because the machine was only meant to go forward (and fast as possible), an array of gauges was not necessary on the Sportmax—just a simple tachometer sufficed.

The NSU Sportmax, which cranked out thirty horsepower and could compete with the blistering 30 fast Italian bikes, is credited for helping launch John Surtees and Mike Hailwood to stardom.

1955 NSU SPORTMAX SPECIFICATIONS:

Engine type:
Air-cooled, SOHC single

Displacement:
247 cubic centimeters

Horsepower:
30

Special feature:
Sophisticated, lightweight, small capacity racing single with soon-to-be-banned "dustbin" fairing (deemed too dangerous in side winds).

CHAPTER 26

1955 AJS 7R

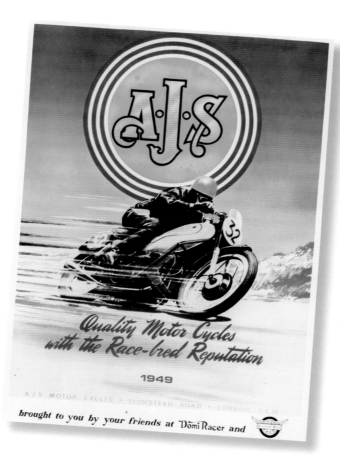

A. J. Stevens Company (its products branded AJS) was founded in 1909 in Wolverhampton, England, and made contributions to motorcycle history alongside its partner Matchless motorcycles. Joe Stevens and his sons, who owned Stevens Screw Company, started building motorcycles and engines before the turn of the century in 1897. When one of their engines (a side-valve single installed in a Wearwell motorcycle) landed a podium finish in a twenty-four-hour endurance event, the senior Stevens decided to go racing.

The company started building 300cc production singles and set its sights on the Isle of Man. By 1914, its 350cc racers had claimed four of the top five spots in the TT junior. Business changed during World War 1, when the company switched to building munitions for the British army. But production of 350s resumed after the war, and Cyril Williams, riding an AJS, went on to win the Junior TT in 1920. (The bike was reported to have broken down at the end of the race and had to be pushed home by Williams.) Riders on AJS bikes took the first four places in the Junior TT in 1921 and a first-place Senior finish—a race meant for 500s—by rider Howard Davies.

The company produced a wide array of motorcycles for the public in 250, 350, 500, and 1,000cc displacements, including singles and twins, roadsters, tourers, commercial vehicles, racers, and sidecars. All this variety may have had the deleterious effect of stretching the company thin. While

AJS introduced a new chain-driven overhead cam 350cc single racer in 1948. Named the 7R, it quickly came to hold court at races at all levels including the Manx and Grand Prix.

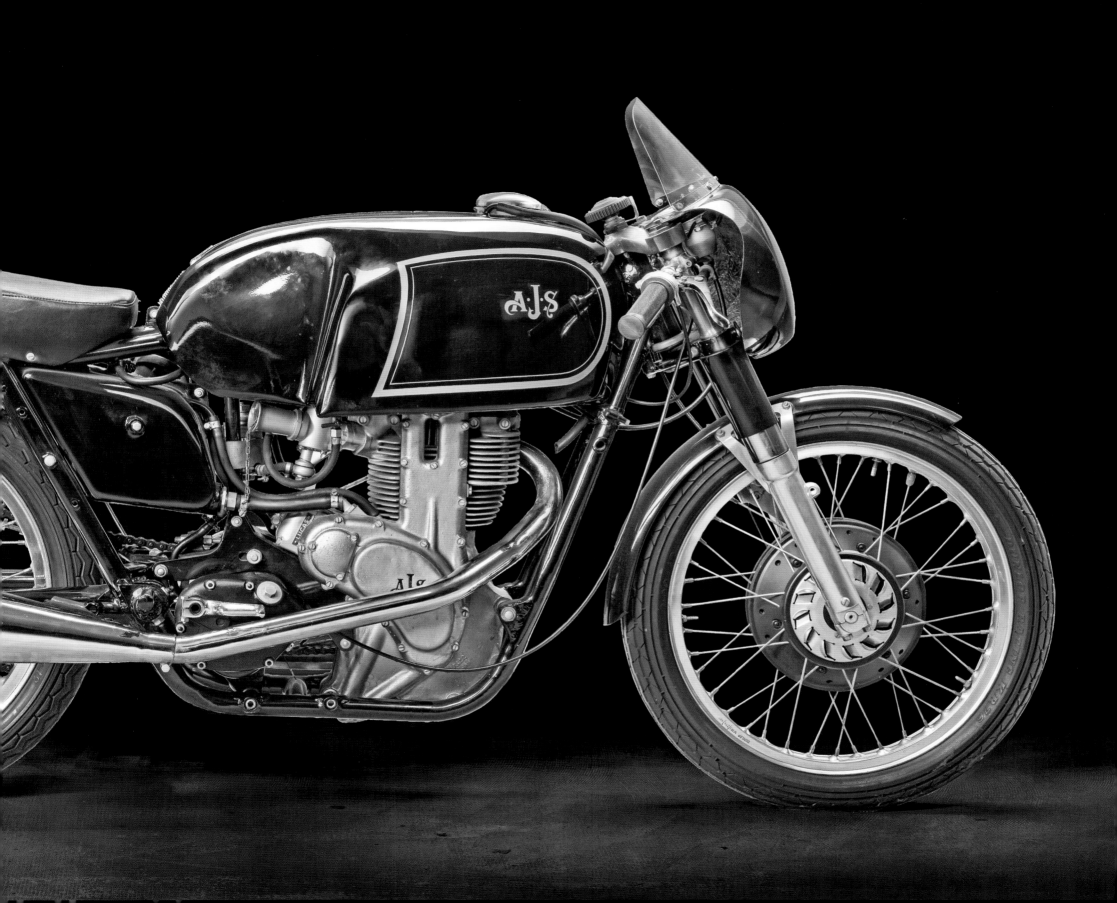

To keep breakdowns to a minimum and speed up the 7R during roadraces and pit stops, the chain oiler could feed the rollers while the bike was in motion at over 110 miles per hour.

Right: The tanks were thinned for aerodynamics, the cylinder well-exposed for cooling, and the brakes powerful and capable—the 1955 AJS 7R came from the factory ready to race.

dabbling also with cars and buses, A. J. Stevens went bankrupt after the stock market crashed.

AJS was taken over by Matchless in 1931, and the now-dual firm became Associated Motor Cycles (AMC) by 1938, producing similar or identical bikes with different badges and features, to capitalize on enthusiasm for both types of bikes. Moving forward, the company attempted to compete with BMW's supercharged racers, which included building a liquid-cooled, supercharged V-four, but these bikes were ultimately unsuccessful. They did, however, produce smooth, comfortable roadsters such as the postwar Model 30, a 600cc twin that was reliable and popular enough to keep AMC going well into the mid-1960s.

After the war, AJS made its name known again in 1949 with a victory in the first FIM 500cc world championship with the E-95, a 500cc twin previously known as the Porcupine, ridden to victory by Leslie Graham. Originally designed by Joe Craig and Harry Collier to be supercharged, the Porcupine had to be retrofitted to accommodate the 1946 ban on superchargers in the world championship. The original bike got its name from its cooling "fins," which were an unconventional design that looked more like spikes. AJS motorcycles continued to be competitive

into the 1950s with its 350cc "Boy Racer" Model 7R, which was later enlarged to 500cc and marketed as the Matchless G50. Gradually, the AJS and Matchless motorcycles faded from view, both in racing and in public, in the wake of superior British, then Italian, then Japanese competition.

The AJS name has managed to live on in a subtle way. As early as the late 1960s, the Norton-Villiers group started producing two-stroke racers and off-road bikes, which found a special place in amateur road racing, trials, and scrambles. Today the AJS company serves mostly as a distributor of small-displacement learner bikes and scooters manufactured in China.

To streamline the AJS 7R for race applications, the fuel and oil tanks were slimmed to reduce frontal area and height, making the bike equally fast and beautiful.

1955 AJS 7R SPECIFICATIONS:

Engine type:
Air-cooled, SOHC single

Displacement:
348 cubic centimeters

Horsepower:
32

Special feature:
Affordable, conventional, workmanlike club racer with a surprising turn of speed, earning it the nickname "Boy Racer."

PART III

The Art of Speed

The motorcycling world took quite a while to recover after World War II. People had more important things to worry about, such as survival, and the development of something as impractical as motorcycles took a back seat to staying alive.

But once the base needs of food and shelter were met, people turned their attention to meta needs such as motorcycles and racing. While the war had been a tragedy of unimaginable scope in terms of human suffering, it had also been the most intense driver of technology the world had ever seen, and by the mid-1950s that technology was being applied to motorcycles. The result was that motorcycle performance took a quantum leap in the postwar years. Motorcycles that would do the ton—100 miles per hour, once the exclusive domain of the racing community— became available to average riders. The world had developed a taste for the thrill of speed, and motorcycle manufacturers were only too happy to sate that desire.

CHAPTER 27

1955 Triumph TR5 and 1959 Bonneville

What's in a name? The word *Triumph* is applied to the engineering company (and its benefactors, descendants, and replacements) and its products, but could as well describe the story of Triumph motorcycles, which arrived in this world just after 1900 and continues to this day—one of the longest running motorcycle makes in history. Triumph embodies the spirit and the art of youthful rebellion.

The New Triumph Company, originally founded in Coventry, England, in 1889, relocated to Meridan after World War II, and today is centered in Hinckley. The company got started by two German gents, Siegfried Bettmann and Mauritz Schulte, in the late 1800s building bicycles. Rapid developments in fuels and combustion engines prompted the company to start building motorcycles, which had suddenly become profitable.

Their first attempt was a bicycle fitted with a Belgian engine. Its modest success, and Triumph's hunger for speed, led the company to begin building complete motorcycles under its own badge in 1905. The factory lovingly produced 500cc and 550cc four-stroke singles, such as the Roadster, TT, H, and SD. When World War I broke out, it was Triumph that supplied the Allied military with motorcycles, most notably the Model H, fondly remembered by soldiers as the "trusty Triumph."

The 1955 Triumph TR5—the Trophy—was a street machine designed for trials riding. Bikes exactly like this one won multiple ISDTs and became worldwide phenomenons.

During the 1920s, Triumph's massive factories manufactured upwards of thirty thousand bikes and cars a year. Unfortunately, the Great Depression dealt a heavy series of blows to the company, requiring the sale of its German motorcycle counterpart in Nuremburg (which continued to build Triumphs until the late 1950s) and its bicycle works, which were taken in by the Raleigh company. Even with these stopgaps, the company went bankrupt by the mid-1930s, its car division scooped up by Standard Motors, and its motorcycle unit bought by Jack Sangster, who also owned Ariel.

It was during this time Edward Turner appeared at Triumph. Under Sangster in 1928, Turner had signed on with Ariel after designing and submitting the engine that became the Square Four. Ariel went bankrupt a few years later, and Sangster bought the company and made Turner chief designer. When in 1936 Sangster bought Triumph too, he changed the

Continued on page 172

Left: A favorite of Hollywood types for hooligan credibility, *Rebel Without a Cause* actor James Dean owned a Triumph TR5 Trophy just like this one. So did Fonzie (*Happy Days*).

Opposite page: The 1955 Triumph Trophy TR5 is a 500cc bike evolved from the Speed Twin—light as the 350, but exceptionally powerful in its Trophy trim.

1955 TRIUMPH TR5 TROPHY SPECIFICATIONS:

Engine type:
Air-cooled, vertical, OHV parallel twin

Displacement:
498 cubic centimeters

Horsepower:
33

Special feature:
High pipes, fork gaiters, and chromed tank rack gave the right look and feel.

Triumph had designed the 1959 Bonneville like the Thunderbird, with a headlight nacelle and full fenders. Rainy-day English riders liked it; Americans didn't care for it.

Continued from page 169

name to Triumph Engineering Company, appointing Turner, at the fresh young age of thirty-five, chief designer and general manager.

Sales lagged during the Depression, but found new life after the owner discovered a market for its bikes in the United States.

With the focus of designer Edward Turner, energy and enthusiasm once again took hold and the company started producing popular and profitable bikes. Turner converted the then-current Triumph lineup of 250, 350, and 500cc singles into the Tiger 70, 80, and 90, all sporty roadsters with upswept pipes, polished engine bits, fresh paint colors, and chrome fuel tanks. The numbers 70, 80, and 90 referred to the speeds the bikes were claimed to be able to attain. The singles were eye catching, cheap to produce, and easy to maintain. Triumph had found a winner.

A year later, Turner introduced the Speed Twin, a fast, solid piece of work (which sold for only £75 pounds at the time) that set a precedent for Triumph design for decades. It was lighter than the Tiger 90 with a more powerful engine, making it a sport bike that could break the 90 mile-per-hour barrier. Production of Triumph motorcycles went all-military with the Triumph 3HW at the onset of World War II; unfortunately, Germans destroyed the factory building in the Blitz in 1940. Much of the machinery and equipment was salvaged and moved to Meridan, and Triumph returned to production shortly after the war ended.

Most of the bikes produced immediately after the war went to the United States. Triumph produced the 500cc Speed Twin, Tiger 100, and Trophy in great numbers and business thrived. The Speed Twin and the Tiger were newly available with telescopic forks in an optional sprung hub, Triumph's first attempt at rear suspension. The original design surfaced before World War II, but was not put into production until operations resumed in 1946. Pity that it hadn't been destroyed in the Blitz in 1940. This curious feature, sourced from aircraft designs, contained a plunger-type rear suspension unit contained entirely within the rear hub, which added 17 pounds to the hub's weight and offered about 2 inches of spring travel. Not only was the design inadequate for the bikes' weight and handling needs, it was considered a dangerous failure—one of the first known instances of a motorcycle component with a safety warning cast into it. Still, Triumph offered this option on its bikes until 1955.

Late 1940s and early 1950s racing wins for Triumph bikes among amateurs and in International Six Days Trials meant steady demand for 500cc Triumph twins, including the new Grand Prix and Trophy models. Turner decided the way to win American hearts was with more displacement and cushier ride, and introduced the Thunderbird in 1949, a bored-out Speed Twin in a 650cc touring package. He was right—the United States groped for the bike by the thousands. Marlon Brando rode a T-Bird in *The Wild One*, generating great publicity for Triumph but a rather regrettable hooligan image for motorcycles and their riders that never quite went away. As a side bonus, the Thunderbird holds the honor of having set fire to the hearts of police motor officers worldwide, who took the bikes in for active police duty. This is interesting because the T-bird was intended to be the "tame" Triumph motorcycle; the new Tiger 100 (and 110) was meant to be the high-powered sport bike—motor cops in the day preferred to have the fastest machines available. Ironically, it was a modified Thunderbird that set the unofficial motorcycle land-speed record of 214 miles per hour and held it for fifteen years until about 1970. Legendary folk rock singer Bob Dylan owned a 1964 Triumph Tiger 100. He missed several tours after crashing it in 1966.

The Birmingham Small Arms Company (BSA), a conglomerate of industrial manufacturing businesses, acquired Triumph in the early 1950s. When Sangster sold Triumph to BSA in 1951, he took a seat on the

Right: The Bonneville, when introduced in 1958, was a groundbreaking bike. It went on to be one of Triumph's best sellers.

The 1959 Bonneville's stock carburetors shared a common, remote float bowl mounted to the frame. This design caused stalling under hard braking. Owners swapped out the carbs for better performance.

board of directors and saw to the appointment of Edward Turner as chief executive for BSA's entire automotive division (at the time, Daimler and Carbodies), which also comprised the motorcycle companies Ariel, BSA, and Triumph.

Business was booming. In 1954, Triumph finally mated a swingarm rear suspension to its bikes, creating another wave of success. These bikes were so popular and sporty that Harley-Davidson was forced to jump in and compete head-to-head with Triumph, and introduced the 883 Sportster as a result. The Bonnie still ran circles around the American competition, though sales of the Sportster were phenomenal and continue to this day.

In 1958 Triumph and Turner's most legendary design was unveiled in the form of the Bonneville T120. The bike was an instant hit: a test rider reached almost 130 miles per hour in a publicity event. Turner, however, was nonplussed and feared the Bonneville would be the death knell for Triumph motorcycles. He was wrong. The Bonneville went on to become one of the most popular Triumph motorcycles of all time.

Triumph enjoyed a nice honeymoon period under BSA as the biggest manufacturer of motorcycles in the world, before some poor business decisions in the face of German, Italian, and Japanese competition left Turner and Triumph nearly for dead by the early 1970s. In 1957, Turner and Triumph started producing motorcycles with enclosed rears that buyers unaffectionately referred to as bathtubs. These proved to be a significant mistake for BSA and Triumph. The styling was phased out and eventually gone by the mid-1960s, but it left a chink in the armor of a mighty company that shook the public's confidence. The bathtub fairings, quality problems, labor troubles, and other management slips left BSA in financial dire straits.

During the 1960s, the demand for motorcycles opened the door to the more technologically advanced and cheaper bikes from Japan. Apparently, Turner toured several Japanese motorcycle factories and was shaken by the scope of production and competition evident in Japan. Turner retired in 1963. Poor choices (the Tina and Tigress scooters), poor designs (broken frames, leaking cases, unreliable electrical systems),

and inefficient production processes notwithstanding, the company continued to advance their name with unit construction and more power, culminating in a production class win at the 1969 Isle of Man TT for a Bonneville.

Among the new offerings in the late 1960s was the new triple, the three-cylinder, 750cc Trident. (Triumph's parent company BSA was also producing the same basic triple, called the Rocket 3.) The triples made phenomenal racers, winning multiple titles before being eclipsed by the Japanese two-strokes. The Trident was faster and more agile than its competition, but was plagued with quality and reliability problems compared to the Japanese bikes—and then Honda released the CB 750. Riders the world over started migrating to the Honda and Kawasaki camp's more advanced bikes as Triumph, mired in tradition and social pressures, continued to struggle.

In the early 1970s, BSA went bankrupt. The company resurfaced under the management of the Norton-Villers group, which owned AJS, Matchless, and other well-known British marques. The new Norton-Villiers-Triumph (NVT) group meant to forge ahead building bikes, but the consolidation and resulting factory closures and layoffs disrupted any chance NVT had of regaining a grip on its bikes' commercial success. NVT tried to close the Meriden plant, but the workers kept it open, creating a labor cooperative that continued to churn out 750 Bonnevilles and Tigers, even as NVT collapsed in the late 1970s. The co-op obtained the rights to the Triumph name and continued to produce new bikes, keeping a respectable market share in the United Kingdom but no longer able to compete elsewhere. By 1983, Triumph was again bankrupt.

Yet, there was still a spark of life. To keep the brand alive, a wealthy enthusiast named John Bloor bought the rights to the company and continued to produce, on a relatively microscopic scale, a few Triumph motorcycles through the 1980s—just to say that Triumph production never actually "stopped." Then in the early 1990s, Bloor produced the results of eight years of hard design work: modern Triumph motorcycles ready to launch the company into the twenty-first century. Among the new releases were

old favorites such as the Trident and the Trophy (now a four), followed shortly by a Speed Triple, Daytona, and a new Thunderbird. Before long, the company was again producing Tigers and Bonnevilles, and the metamorphosis was complete. Triumph Motorcycles Limited, now based in Hinckley, England, has once again become one of the most prolific and respected motorcycle manufacturers in the world.

1959 TRIUMPH T120 BONNEVILLE SPECIFICATIONS:

Engine type:
Air-cooled, vertical, OHV parallel twin

Displacement:
649 cubic centimeters

Horsepower:
46

Special feature:
Headlamp nacelle: The British market loved it, the North American market did not.

CHAPTER 28

1957 Maico Typhoon

Maicowerk was a West German bicycle and accessory company founded by Ulrich Maitsch, and later taken over by sons Otto and Wilhelm Maitsch, which began building motorcycle engines as early as 1926. Its first offerings in the internal combustion world were mostly small displacement two-stroke singles. After World War II, the company began producing complete motorcycles, scooters, and even microcars.

During the 1950s, Maico recognized there was money to be made in supplying simple transportation devices to the masses and quickly released the 250cc Blizzard and the 400cc Typhoon. Both were startlingly beautiful motorcycles, the Blizzard looking more like a traditional motorcycle akin to the DKW RT125, whereas the Typhoon was much more futuristic, an art deco take on German engineering.

Maico also jumped on the scooter bandwagon. After first trying the Maicomobil, a two-wheeled vehicle that resembled a car (enthusiasts and detractors alike referred to it as "The Dustbin"), Maico added to the lineup the Maicoletta, a bathtub-looking contraption quite similar to the bikes that were tried and failed from BSA, Ducati, and Triumph. At the time, with its 250cc two-stroke engine, the bike was one of the biggest scooters in the world—heavy and fast, capable of 70 miles per hour, with four speeds, front and rear drum brakes, an enclosed drive, and Bosch electric pendulum starter, which started the bike by rotating the crankshaft gently back and forth.

In the 1960s and '70s, with street bike production looking like a dead end, the company made an about shift and began building bikes to be used off-road—the dirt bike craze had begun and was dominated by the likes of CZ, Husqvarna, and, quickly, Maico. In the early days of the eastern invasion, before the Japanese had really gotten their wheels under them, Maico produced legendary, loveable, and competitive motocross bikes that destroyed the competition. Vintage off-road motorcycle enthusiasts' most prestigious prize in the twenty-first century is coming across an original Maico enduro bike for sale.

The success of Maico's off-road machines lasted for twenty years, until some unexpected financial and quality problems sounded the death knell in the mid-1980s. After two consecutive years in which their bikes literally fell apart at the seams—unprecedented power but no chassis and suspension to manage it—and in the face of the now unstoppable Japanese competition, the company quietly folded and passed into motorcycling history. Many of their motocross bikes are still in use in competition today, as trusted, reliable friends that go exactly where you point them, bounce just how you want them, and turn precisely when you need them.

The Typhoon's innovative and futuristic engine case and other parts blend with the swoopy, art-deco-style bathtub bodywork.

Opposite page: This 1957 Maico Typhoon is a 400cc, two-stroke twin. At nearly 400 pounds, it was not a lightweight, but the little twin could power the machine up to 80 miles per hour.

1957 MAICO TYPHOON SPECIFICATIONS:

Engine type:
Air-cooled 2-stroke twin

Displacement:
395 cubic centimeters

Horsepower:
22.5

Special feature:
Art Deco-style bathtub bodywork was all the rage in the late 1950s.

CHAPTER 29

1959 MV DOHC 125 and 1965 350

L ike many Italian makes of its time, MV Agusta's foremost interest was building race bikes. Street bikes—MV fours for the masses—were a necessary side business.

The idea for Meccanica Verghera (MV) motorcycles came from two brothers, Vincenzo and Domenico Agusta, trying to save the family business. Originally a builder and designer of helicopters near Milan, the Agusta firm was in trouble and at risk of putting its factory workers out on the street. The brothers, who had a taste for racing, cooked up a plan to supply the world with cheap transportation, save their employees' jobs, and use the proceeds to finance their racing habit.

Their plan worked, and the tiny street bikes they produced en masse bankrolled the development of some of the most successful race bikes the world has ever seen. MV Agusta's first bike, a 100cc two-stroke single, was an instant success on the racetrack and the street. What followed for twenty years were mostly 100–200cc café racers and scooters, such as the Turismo and Turismo Rapido, Pullman and Superpullman, the Raid, Chicco, Liberty, and Arno.

Alongside this supply of beautiful, simple, and cheap streetbikes came a supply of beautiful, simple, and expensive race bikes. The 1950s racetracks were dominated by MV's 125 and 250cc singles; racing in the late 1950s through the early 1970s was dominated

by MV's 350 and 500cc twins, triples, and fours. The brilliant red and silver machines, through the factory team and private racers, won Isle of Man TT titles thirty-four times in various classes, the 350cc world championship ten times, and the 500cc world championship seventeen times *in a row* from 1956 to 1974.

The engine that made all this possible was the eight-valve, 350 and 500cc, dual-overhead-cam inline four, an indirect result of its engineer Pietro Remor's experience designing the Gilera 500cc Four. Comparable in power and prowess to the two-strokes of the 1970s, these bikes could spin up to 14,000 rpm and generate more than 100 horsepower, in a package weighing barely 300 pounds. John Surtees raced these bikes to numerous world championships before retiring in 1960.

Giacomo Agostini, legendary rider for MV Agusta, is widely recognized as the greatest Grand Prix rider of all time. His career spanned almost twenty years, during which time Ago won fifteen world Grand Prix titles, twelve Isle of Man TT titles, and an astonishing 122 Grands Prix races, rarely making a mistake

This 1959 MV Agusta Bialbero 125 was a four-stroke single with dual overhead cams, telescopic fork, swingarm with dual shocks, and drum brakes front and rear.

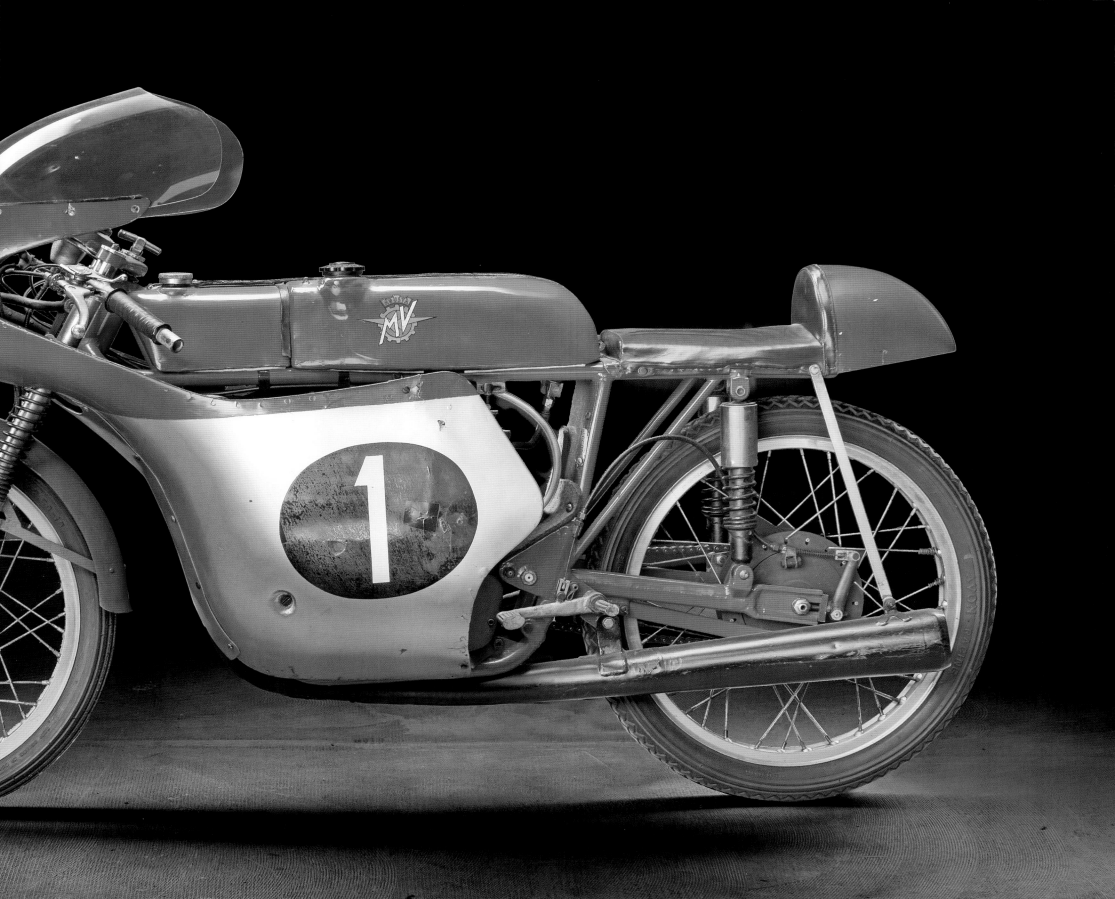

during the entire time. Agostini was motorcycling's first real international superstar; for years he appeared undefeatable on the grid. Ago learned from fellow MV rider and mentor Mike Hailwood's move to Honda, after which Ago completely dominated for MV, on both the 500cc and 350cc from 1968 to 1972. In 1973 Ago won the 350cc title one last time for MV, then moved to Yamaha to win the 350cc championship in 1974 and the 500cc championship in 1975.

As bikes started getting bigger in the 1960s and sales of smaller bikes declined, MV Agusta began producing larger bikes in smaller numbers. Unfortunately, the street bikes the factory produced for the public were never as heart stopping as the race bikes. They were decent bikes, but not pretty compared to their racing counterparts, and nearly as expensive. Fewer sales meant less money available for race development, and when Domenico, the driving force behind the company's motorcycle business, died in the early 1970s, the firm refocused and dropped motorcycles from its production schedule by 1980.

The MV Agusta name, like many others that didn't survive the Japanese competition in the 1970s, enjoyed a modest revival starting in the 1990s. The Cagiva group bought the rights to the name and built some stunning 750–1,000cc F4 sport bikes in the traditional red-and-silver livery. Unable to remain profitably in business, Cagiva was bought up by a carmaker, and the manufacturing rights bounced from owner to owner for several years before Cagiva finally set up shop again in Varese, Italy. Now focused on building MVs, the company has resumed production of a very limited supply of expensive, breathtaking motorcycles.

In the twenty-first century, there is enough demand worldwide for limited production, boutique-quality superbikes that marques such as MV Agusta are back in business. As the average age of motorcycle enthusiasts in the western hemisphere has reached the fifties, the money and the memories to rationalize such a purchase seems to remain in good supply.

Below: Alongside the Meccanica Verghera (MV) supply of beautiful, simple, and cheap streetbikes in the 1950s came a supply of beautiful, simple, and expensive 125-250cc racebikes.

Right: Tiny and lightweight but deadly effective, the Bialbero used four gears and 12,000 rpm to generate 20 horsepower that propelled the 175-pound bike up to 125 miles per hour.

1959 MV BIALBERO 125 SPECIFICATIONS:

Engine type:
Air-cooled, DOHC single

Displacement:
124 cubic centimeters

Horsepower:
20

Special feature:
Highly developed and lightweight, this high-revving double-overhead cam single was built on the same platform as all the MV World Championship bikes.

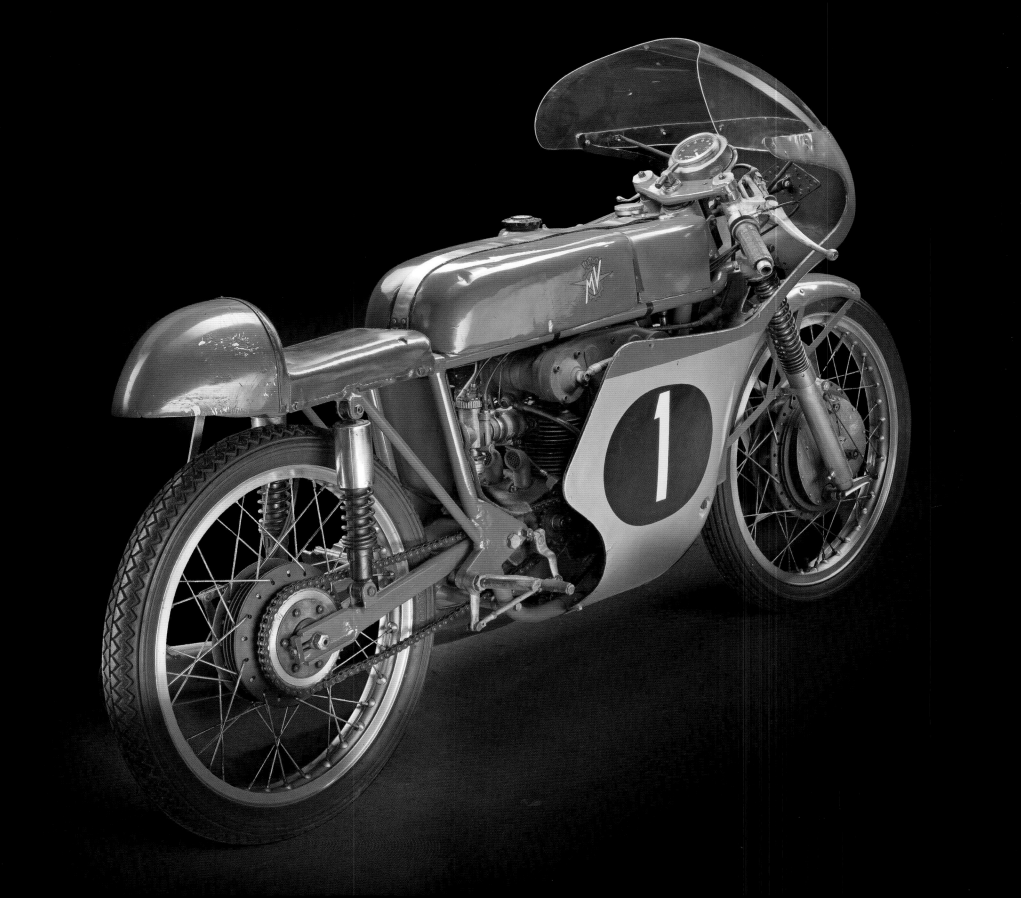

Above: The MV 350 triple evolved into the 500 triple, arguably the finest racing motorcycle of all time. Giacomo Agostini rode the MV Agusta 500cc triple to *seven* consecutive 500cc Grand Prix world championships starting in 1966.

Opposite page: When Honda became seriously competitive withits RC143, MV developed the 125cc single-race platform into 350 and 500cc machines.

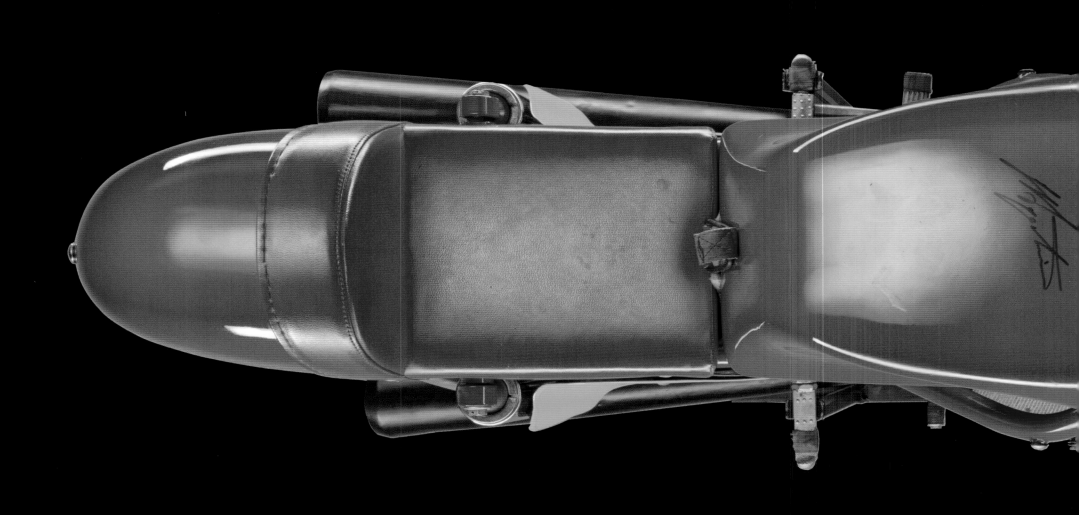

Previous pages: Legendary racer Phil Read was a master of understatement: "No bike is perfect to a rider who's pushing to the absolute limit, but the Three was a very good bike."

Right: Debuting in 1965, the original triple (a 350) was faster than MV's old 500cc four and was intended to knock newcomer Honda off its throne.

The MV triple was a tiny, four-stroke 350 that cranked out 72 horsepower. Its short wheelbase of 52 inches gave it great maneuverability.

1965 MV 350 THREE SPECIFICATIONS:

Engine type:
Air-cooled, DOHC in-line 3-cylinder

Displacement:
350 cubic centimeters

Horsepower:
70 or more

Special feature:
First year of the classic MV 350 3-cylinder and the base for the 500cc GP bike.

CHAPTER 30

1960 JAWA Factory Racer and JAWA Ice Racer

Simple, practical bikes, Jawas aren't fancy, but they are fun to ride, dependable, and retro-attractive. And you can have them in most any color you like, as long as it's red. One of the longest-lived and subtly famous motorcycle manufacturers was established by František Janecek in Prague. Since 1929, when Janecek purchased the motorcycle division of the German company Wanderer, the products of this company have been known as JAWA—a combination of the names Jane⊠ek and Wanderer.

Frantisek Janecek came from a small village in Bohemia in former Czechoslovakia. As a young man, he studied mechanical engineering and had his own shop in Prague. After World War I, he found his stride and started building things, eventually nailing down more than fifty patents for his work, including the well-known Janecek hand grenade. Unfortunately, armaments between the World War I and World War II were not a profitable business, so Janecek took notice of the popularity of motorcycles and decided to try his hand at it.

While he wasn't a designer of motorcycles per se, he had an exceptional grasp of mass production techniques. He sourced an engine design from the German Wanderer company in 1929, at the same time Wanderer was looking to unload its motorcycle division in the wake of competition from BMW and DKW. He started with a 500cc bike that was solidly built and sold well right away.

Sensing a mass-transportation opportunity, he enlisted a 175cc Villiers two-stroke single to create a light and simple commuter bike that was half the cost of the more common 500cc bikes and 750cc machines sporting sidecars. The little JAWA was so popular in Czechoslovakia in the 1930s that JAWA dropped its 500cc machines. Also built during that time was the tiny 100cc Robot, which was an early example of unit construction in which the engine case and gearbox formed one unit. Next came JAWA's 350cc four-strokes, the first engines developed in-house, in the mid-1930s.

But World War II interrupted development and production of civilian products. The Germans occupying the country demanded that JAWA produce

In 1949, JAWA merged with a competitor (CZ) and both companies came under communist control. Still, the firm was able to create memorable street and factory race bikes.

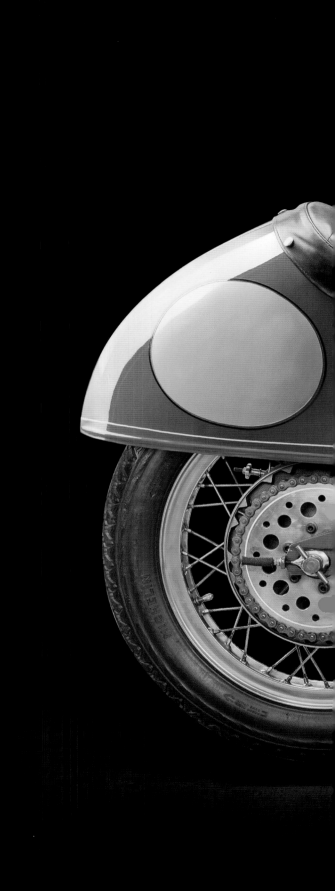

aircraft and generator engines. However, the JAWA technicians, in the best interest of the Third Reich of course, were keen to produce a "people's machine," and they were allowed to design and test a new model in relative secrecy. When the war was over, JAWA immediately returned to motorcycle production and was the first to start selling bikes again in Europe—to a world hungry for personal transportation. The company's new two-stroke 250cc bike with rear suspension was ready to go. Soon, its larger 350cc brother joined it on the assembly line and business was good.

Jawa, which has produced more than three million motorcycles in its lifespan, was able to capitalize on solid construction to create reliable race machines on a limited budget.

1960 JAWA 500 FACTORY ROAD RACER SPECIFICATIONS:

Engine type:
Air-cooled, DOHC parallel twin

Displacement:
500 cubic centimeters

Horsepower:
45

Special feature:
Czechoslovakian origin with little-motorcycle road-racing heritage.

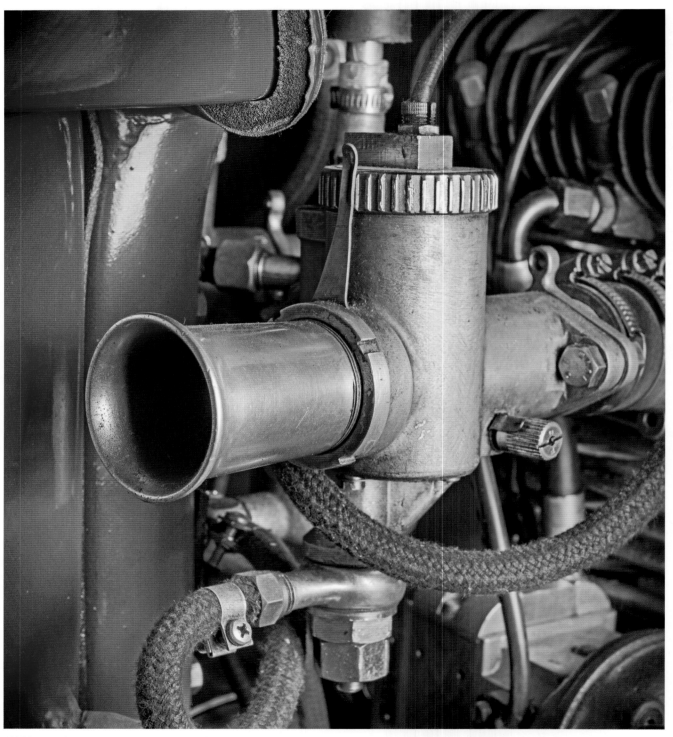

JAWA used its popular and reliable 500cc air-cooled parallel twin design (lightened and tuned to create a beautiful and swift roadracer) to compete on a minimal scale in the 1960s.

JAWA's real race dominance came in speedway, dirt track, and ice racing, where its four-stroke engines still hold an advantage in competition.

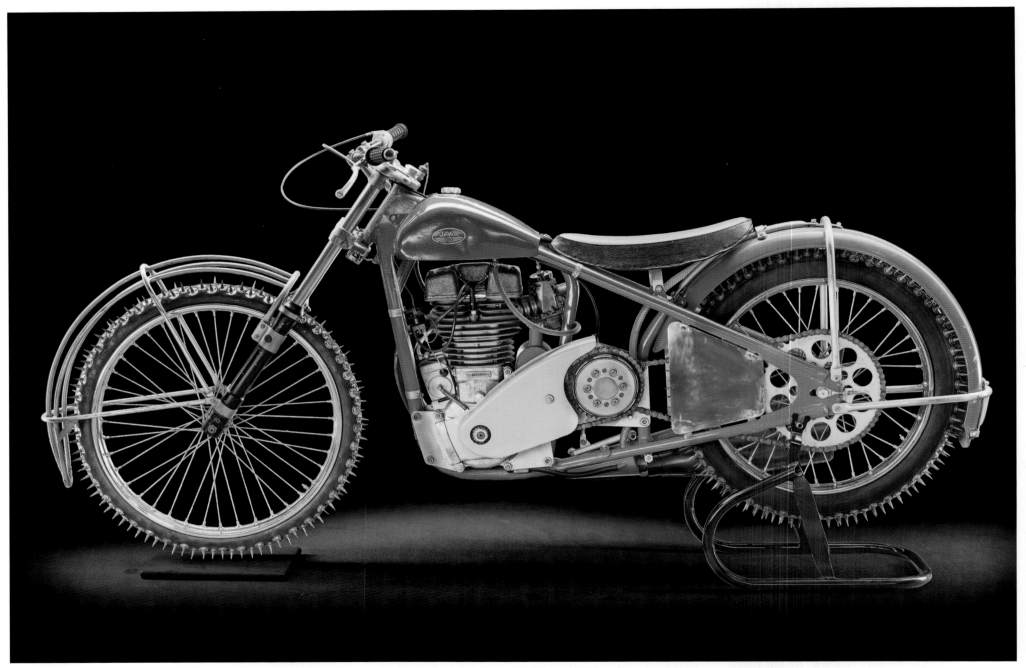

Because of their smooth power delivery and awesome, four-stroke power, JAWA motorcycles have been competitive on oval tracks for nearly fifty years.

Push-start the JAWA ice racer to get it going. There is no "neutral" and only one gear: Forward and fast. Use a dry clutch to get forward progress started—after that, it's all gas.

With the nationalization of the country in 1945, and the dominance of English, German, and Italian bikes notwithstanding, the company continued to produce small-displacement motorcycles for the common man for forty years, eventually creating a distribution network that encompassed more than 120 countries. JAWA motorcycles adorned roadways throughout the world; more than three million units were built, until production scaled back in the late 1980s. Since then, JAWA has quietly and efficiently set to producing a limited array of commuter bikes in the 50–350cc range and a series of 650cc Rotax-engined bikes, including an adventure bike called the Sportard.

In a bike that weighs less than 200 pounds, the horsepower this alcohol-fueled single puts out makes you feel as if you're riding some kind of monster.

CIRCA 1984 JAWA ICE RACER SPECIFICATIONS:

Engine type:
Air-cooled, OHV single cylinder

Displacement:
500 cubic centimeters

Horsepower:
51

Special feature:
Two-speed gearbox with no neutral and no brakes.

CHAPTER 31

1963 Honda CR93, 1966 CB450, 1970 CB750 KO, and 1992 NR750

Motorcycling and motorcycle manufacturing changed as the 1960s ended. The pivot point was 1969, when Honda introduced the CB750.

Honda started life as a manufacturer of piston rings for Toyota. The company's founder Soichiro Honda, a racing enthusiast, built and raced his own cars before taking an interest in two-wheeled speed. Motorcycles quickly became Honda's passion.

After World War II, the world was hungry for cheap transportation. The Honda Technical Research Institute—twelve guys working in a garage—started building motorized bicycles with 50cc generator engines left over from the war. When the supply of ready-made engines ran out, they started building and selling small engines for customers to attach to their own bicycles. In 1949—relatively late in motorcycle history—Soichiro Honda liquidated his business and incorporated the Honda Motor Company. The company built its first proprietary motorcycle, the

100cc Model D (better known as the Dream) later that year. The Dream sparked a bigger dream: Honda decided in the 1950s that his bikes could win races and set to work making that dream a reality. This was a big gamble for Honda, because to focus on racing was to distract from serving the hungry masses, but it paid off. By 1960, Honda bikes were competing successfully in the Isle of Man TT and the world championship series.

Honda was a savvy marketer. When the company decided to sell bikes in the United States, it created a positive, good-clean-fun kind of marketing campaign to drum up interest in its product. Far from the antisocial, leather-clad hooligans terrorizing the townsfolk and staring luridly at our daughters,

Not always the fastest, these bikes won because they could *finish* races. The sound from the dual pipes was reported to be "hostile" and "outrageous" for a 125.

Honda depicted a different kind of motorcyclist with the "You meet the nicest people on a Honda" campaign. This campaign was so successful that Honda eventually became the largest motorcycle manufacturer in the world.

At the same time, Honda's bikes were winning races, particularly in the smaller classes. Its 125, 250, and 350cc twins, fours, and sixes were at the top of the podium in world championships, thanks to Mike Hailwood. Hailwood was probably the best-known racer campaigning Hondas at the time. After representing Ducati in the 1950s, "Mike the Bike" rode for Honda, battling head to head with his archrival Giacomo Agostini. He made early waves in the 250cc world championship, riding a four-cylinder four-stroke Honda.

These little wonders were fast, reliable, and expensive: At $1,400 in 1963, a CR93 was a serious investment when average income was maybe $6,000 a year.

The 1963 Honda CR93 was a 125cc production racing parallel twin, with dual overhead cams, eight valves, and a tiny crank and pistons that could spin up to 12,000 rpm and reach 100 miles per hour.

She's loaded

Santa's Helper

She's smooth, svelte, yet kind of comfy.
Twist her throttle and she responds to the utmost of her twin cylinder, 4-stroke OHC engine. Her 4-speed transmission never misses a mesh.
At 10,500 rpm 16.5 reindeer are in there prancin' and dancin'—

horns and all. Add to that a 150cc capacity, and an 8:1 compression ratio and you'll know what makes Santa go ho, ho, ho.
She's a self starter, too. Which saves a man a lot of trouble. Want her number? It's Honda CA-95.
If the line's busy, you can get the address of your nearest dealer

or other information, by writing American Honda Motor Co., Inc., Department DM, 100 W. Alondra, Gardena, California.

HONDA
world's biggest seller!

1963 HONDA CR93 SPECIFICATIONS:

Engine type:
Air-cooled, DOHC parallel twin

Displacement:
125 cubic centimeters

Horsepower:
16.5

Special feature:
Sophisticated twin that was both fast and reliable, and notably noisy.

Soichiro Honda was a racer at heart. Motorcycles were Honda's first passion and lifelong love—the company didn't start building cars until 1963.

Honda's first big bike was the "Black Bomber," a 450 twin that attempted, not quite successfully, to compete with the bigger British twins. The Brit bikes were bigger and faster, but the Honda proved itself to be more reliable, smoother, and more comfortable—and it didn't leak oil. These attributes kept it popular with the public and opened the door to the event that changed motorcycling more than any other: the introduction of the CB750 in 1969.

It is rumored that when Sorichio Honda began studying American manufacturers to learn how to compete with them, he couldn't believe how *big* the bikes were. Apparently, he must have decided "if you can't beat –me, join –em." The CB750 was like no Japanese or American bike that had come before it. It was the first mass-produced four-cylinder bike,

with electric start, kill switch, turn signals, disc front brake, and an affordable price (about $1,500). More than four hundred thousand of these bikes were sold in its ten-year run. While not an elegant corner carver, it was big, heavy, and fast—just what US riders needed to soak up vast distances at high speeds on rough roads. Smaller bikes derived from the CB's design (the 400 and 500cc versions) were quite popular, and much more sporty due to lighter weight and better handling.

Right: The 1966 Honda Black Bomber (a CB450) was a parallel twin with dual overhead cams also called the Black Hawk. The Bomber was comfortable, smooth, and handled well.

Honda upped the ante with the introduction of the Gold Wing in 1975. The Wing was a big, ponderous touring bike with a smooth and responsive flat-four engine (like two BMW boxer engines bolted together) with liquid cooling. The timing was perfect, as the new riders of the '50s and '60s were just beginning to think they were too old to ride; along came an easy chair that you can ride effortlessly for days on end.

In the mid-1980s, Honda tried to change the motorcycle world again by introducing a V-four sport bike meant to compete with the inline fours in both racing and sport riding. It never did so on a large scale—the inline fours like the Honda CBR are still the sport bike and racing favorites. But the V-four's unique character helped bring the sport-touring tradition to the masses, first with the VFR750 and later with the ST1100. While awesome, limited production bikes such as the RC30 and oval-pistoned NR made waves on the race circuits, the VFR and its bigger brother the ST proved hugely popular on the

Left: Although displacing just 444cc, the Honda CB450 was as fast as Harley Davidson's 900cc Sportster and faster than the 650cc British twins of the day.

Opposite page: Arriving in the mid-1960s, this Black Bomber foreshadowed Honda's desire to build bikes to compete with the British twins that had a hold on the large-displacement market.

1966 HONDA CB450 SPECIFICATIONS:

Engine type:
Air-cooled, DOHC parallel twin

Displacement:
444 cubic centimeters

Horsepower:
43

Special feature:
Nicknamed the Black Bomber, it was faster than the traditional British 650 twins.

street with riders interested in carving corners and logging 500–1,000 miles in a day.

In the early 1990s, Honda's Fireblade, the CBR900RR, altered the trajectory of sport bikes forever. Until then, by today's measures, sport bikes were plenty fast but difficult to handle, with well-designed but poorly suited suspension components—the liter bikes were just too heavy to manage. The driving force behind the project was Tadao Baba, a racer and engineer who had worked for Honda's research and development lab since the 1960s. He created a blueprint of sorts by finally nailing down the right combination of suspension, power, handling, and weight—the 900RR was the first modern sport bike. Baba's goal was to maximize power and handling while keeping to a very, very low maximum weight of about 425 pounds. This brought the Fireblade in at about 5 pounds more than the CBR600. The Fireblade was the first street bike designed by Honda using CAD technology. When the bike was first introduced, test riders were blown away. A rider named Phillip McCallen won the 1996 and 1997 Isle of Man TT production class on a Fireblade—no one had seen anything like it before.

1969 HONDA CB750K0 SPECIFICATIONS:

Engine type:
Air-cooled, SOHC in-line four cylinder

Displacement:
736 cubic centimeters

Horsepower:
51

Special feature:
The bike that stole the "big bike" market from the British and the Americans.

The CB750 never raced well and was quickly outshined by bikes like the Kawasaki Z1, but its size, speed, and comfort made it popular with everyday riders.

Right: The first "universal Japanese motorcycle," most other Japanese bikes for the next ten years looked exactly like the Honda CB750, which permanently altered the motorcycle landscape. The 1970 Honda CB750 held a simple two-valve, single-overhead-cam, 750cc engine with five gears capable of 125 miles per hour.

In the late 1970s, Honda returned to Grand Prix with the NR (new racing) concept. The pinnacle of these designs was the 750cc elliptical-pistoned V-four, the Honda NR.

Left: Although a heavy machine (490 pounds) by modern standards, the engine produced nearly 125 horsepower at 14,000 rpm for superbike speed.

1992 HONDA NR (750) SPECIFICATIONS:

Engine type:
Water-cooled, DOHC V-four with two connecting rods per piston and 32-valve cylinder heads

Displacement:
748 cubic centimeters

Horsepower:
125

Special feature:
Unprecedented complexity with unique elliptical pistons based on the oval piston NR500 Grand Prix racer.

CHAPTER 32

1969 Villa Grand Prix Racer

Brothers Francesco and Walter Villa were accomplished racers, tuners, and builders from Modena, Italy. Moto Villa, an organization still alive today, was a small but significant offshoot of the brothers' passion for two wheels and speed. They were active in the Italian and international road racing championships from the mid-1950s until the early 1970s, when their attentions turned to motocross and enduro machines.

Francesco worked under Fabio Taglioni at Ducati as a race mechanic for the factory team. He went on to race for Ducati, as well as Mondial until the company pulled out of racing in 1957. He went back to Ducati and focused on building and honing racing two-strokes, which included collaborations with Benelli, Moto Guzzi, Montessa, and even Lamborghini in the development of twelve-cylinder Formula 1 competition engines.

In the late 1960s, Francesco and Walter began crafting purpose-built racing prototypes that they believed could compete on the world stage. These were the first, unofficial "Moto Villa" machines. The company started small, in the 125cc class, building air-cooled two-stroke singles with rotary valves that cranked out 30 horsepower. The bikes were intended only for racing and sold to privateers.

They later went on to build 250cc air- and water-cooled two-stroke twins with seven-speed gearboxes

that wrangled close to 40 horsepower, but their first multi-cylinder two-stroke was actually a four-cylinder concept bike.

In 1969 Villa experimented briefly with an early V-four concept that looked great standing still, but was produced a year too late for international competition and never achieved great results at home. The bike's engine consisted of two air-cooled 125cc twins mounted bottom to top at a 30-degree angle with an eight-speed gearbox, rotary valves, and a loop frame. In anticipation of FIM rules, the team limited the gearbox to six speeds, but unanticipated was the FIM's 1970 rule that limited the 250 class to two cylinders or less—a tragic blow to an otherwise promising motorcycle. The brothers attempted to race the bike at home in the Italian Grand Prix, but the bike—still really a prototype—ran erratically during practice and was abandoned for a 250cc single brought as a backup.

By this time, the Villa brothers racing days were nearly over, and Francesco was considered one of the world's foremost experts on two-stroke motorcycle

In true Italian form, the Francesco and Walter Villa one-off race bikes were high-tech, effective, problematic, and unerringly beautiful to look at.

engines. He continued to design and experiment with new engines, but directed his attention toward off-road motocross, endure, and trials applications, a sport that was rapidly becoming popular—and profitable. Villa began building the CR, a motocross bike meant only for racing. His bikes were so well built and competitive, the Villa business expanded to a new facility near Bologna. Next came the FV lineup of off-road bikes, powerful, efficient and lightweight machines that propelled many Italian riders to competitive success and the Villa company to a pronounced, but temporary, commercial success throughout the 1970s and well into the 1980s.

Unfortunately, the 1980s saw the rise of the unstoppable Japanese manufacturers, who were producing reliable, competitive bikes on such a scale that Villa could not compete, financially. Mass production of Villa motorcycles ended, and the company moved back to Modena, where Francesco and his brother could continue to imagine and tinker in the workshop with two-stroke designs. The company still exists today, with the owners experimenting and prototyping engines, and offering technical advice to other builders.

1969 MOTO VILLA 250 GRAND PRIX RACER SPECIFICATIONS:

Engine type:
Air-cooled, rotary valve 2-stroke v-four

Displacement:
250 cubic centimeters

Horsepower:
NA

Special feature:
Courageous engine design combining two 125 twins onto a single crankcase with a 30-degree V angle.

Anticipating FIM rules for six gears or fewer, Walter built the V-4 with only six speeds. Unfortunately, FIM also limited the 250 class to two cylinders, so the bike never saw a Grand Prix race.

Opposite page: This is the original Villa four, acquired from the late Walter Villa's estate. The engine was conceived as two 125cc twins mounted together.

CHAPTER 33

1974 Ducati 750 Sport

Ducati was a horse that started late in the race but came out a winner. The sheer love of motorcycles, apparent in every machine the company builds, is unmistakable. The muscular twins, hyper-sexy frames, and bodywork, and the thrill of the pounding exhaust note send a message that is unmistakably Ducati.

Ducati has had a long and troubled history that includes multiple owners and management agencies, frequent brushes with insolvency, and government rescues. Yet through it all, the company has managed to produce some of the most beautiful, high-performance road bikes the world has ever seen.

The first Ducati products appeared in 1926 when Antonio Cavalieri Ducati and his three sons, Adriano, Bruno, and Marcello, started producing vacuum tubes, condensers, and electrical components in Bologna, Italy. After World War II, motorcycles' popularity as cheap personal transportation in Italy and Europe was at an historic high, and the Ducati company, after missing the first wave of profitable demand, jumped in and started producing a clip-on engine called the Cucciolo ("puppy"), later manufacturing complete motorized bicycles of the same name. These first Ducatis weighed less than 100 pounds and got upwards of 200 miles per gallon—a welcome addition to any Italian household in the early 1950s.

In 1954, famed engineer Fabio Taglioni came on board and propelled Ducati into motorcycling history. Taglioni began his career as a designer for Mondial, supporting the factory's racing effort. Mondial's success earned him quite a reputation, and when he

left, he was said to have entertained job offers from both Ferrari and Ford before committing to work for Ducati. His thirty-five years as master engineer at the company during the golden age of motorcycling made the name Taglioni synonymous with the name Ducati. Taglioni's legend is carefully wrapped with the desmodromic valve design, an artful method of opening and closing the engine valves without the use of conventional coil springs. Desmo valves are closed

In 1974, many race bikes had power and many had great handling. The Ducati Sport boasted both brutal power and sharp, high-speed handling.

mechanically by a camshaft. The desmo design allows for higher engine speeds, more mid-range and top-end power, and reduces friction. The Desmo design cured the high-speed valve float problem created by springs, whose return (to closed) rate would not change no matter how fast the engine was spinning. In 1957, Taglioni created the 125cc Bialbero, the first Ducati to use desmodromic valves. A year later, he introduced a four-cylinder version for Grand Prix racing.

Ducati made an evolutionary leap in 1971 when it released its first twin, the 750 GT, followed soon by the 750 Sport. A 90-degree V-twin, a combination of two ferocious singles using a one crankcase, had its front cylinder thrust forward, nearly parallel to the ground. Ducati debuted the 750SS, which featured desmo valves, at the Imola 200 in 1972. Ducati rider Paul Smart shocked Italy and the world by taking first place in the prestigious race, beating some of the world's top riders, including Giacomo Agostini on an MV Agusta. To add insult to Ago's injury, Bruno Spaggiari placed second on another 750SS, turning the factory race team community on its ear.

Ducatis ridden by Mike Hailwood and Tony Rutter managed five TT Formula 1 world championship wins. Between 1990 and 2011, Ducatis won fourteen World Superbike championships and seventeen manufacturer's world championships, ridden by racing heroes such as Troy Bayliss, Carlos Checa, Troy Corser, Carl Fogarty, Doug Polen, and Raymond Roche. Ducati's dominance does not extend into Moto GP wins, with the notable exception of the blistering performance by Casey Stoner, who won in 2007.

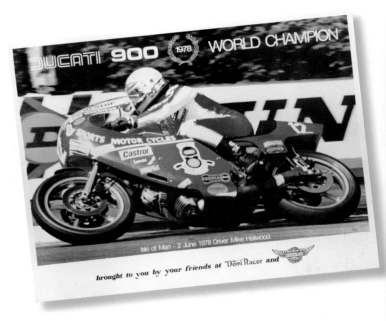

The 750 Sport carried on the Ducati tradition of producing street-legal, thoroughbred racing machines.

1974 DUCATI 750 SPORT SPECIFICATIONS:

Engine type:
Air-cooled, SOHC V-twin

Displacement:
748 cubic centimeters

Horsepower:
64

Special feature:
Bevel drive to camshafts. The Super Sport came with desmodromic valve gear.

Right: The 1974 Ducati Sport was an air-cooled, single-overhead-cam V-twin. The harder you pushed it, the better it behaved. Only 401 were built.

CHAPTER 34

Britten V1000

One of the most remarkable race bikes ever built, the Britten V1000 was the product of essentially one person: John Britten of New Zealand. A talented engineer and artist, he created the Britten Motorcycle Company in the early 1990s and began producing this extraordinary machine. The V1000 is a water-cooled, DOHC, eight-valve, 60-degree, aluminum alloy V-twin pumping out 160-plus horsepower in a package that weighs barely more than 300 pounds. Its design is focused solely on racing. While it looks elaborate, the motorcycle is as minimalist as they come. If ever there was a "rocket engine with wheels and a handlebar," this is it.

This bike had no traditional frame to speak of—the engine, a stressed member, was essentially also the frame. The radiator and rear shock's positions were flip-flopped for centralized mass and space saving: The radiator was under the rider's seat, the rear shock just behind the front wheel. A highly sophisticated suspension kept the wheels on the ground and the power manageable—this bike used a sophisticated engine management and data logging system, monitoring performance so tuners could program as necessary to optimize power. Even the rake and trail were adjustable.

The 1995 Britten V1000 had no traditional frame. The 160-horsepower V-twin was a stressed member serving as the chassis—literally an engine with wheels.

After decades of evolution in performance engines, the Britten V1000 finally made the breakthrough in power-to-weight ratios with extensive use of lightweight carbon fiber.

Right: Only ten Brittens were ever built. Two of them turned the racing world on its head when they took second and third places in the 1991 Daytona Battle of the Twins.

The Britten V1000 was conceived and built solely for racing. The big twin cranked out superbike power in a package that weighed only about 300 pounds.

Opposite page: Before John Britten could full realize his dream at roadracing domination, he died unexpectedly in 1995. This particular Britten, which is number ten, was put together after John Britten died.

1994 BRITTEN V1000 SPECIFICATIONS:

Engine type:
Water-cooled, DOHC V-twin

Displacement:
999 cubic centimeters

Horsepower:
166

Special feature:
Hand built by John Britten and a small team
in Christchurch, New Zealand.

Photographer's Notes

Car photographers have several techniques we can use to "light" the car. I probably am best known as a "light-painting" shooter. Light-painting vehicles is very different from lighting them in a studio with a massive overhead soft box and reflectors. As light-painting maestro Dave Wendt describes it, the process is more organic. I'd add "spontaneous" as well.

When I first started this lighting style, I used a small soft box or even a hardware store work light with an incandescent bulb in it. The lights gave me the control I needed to shine the light on the car to create the image I envisioned. But incandescent bulbs are hot and hard to work with and the bulbs were constantly burning out. Throughout the shoot, if electric power surged or dropped, I had color-shift problems. I tried to use LEDs but they gave me an uneven look with streaks of light in the reflections. I tried other types of lighting to improve the process. I wanted to be cordless, flexible, have even light over the vehicle, and find a lightweight setup that would be easy to handle.

After years of testing light sources I finally found the perfect light system. Cineo Lighting, located in Half Moon Bay, California, manufactures small, easy-to-work-with battery-powered lamps with correct and constant light temperature. Their lamps use remote phosphor technology, not LEDs. Cineo has—for me— the perfect-sized light units to make the perfect image. I shot this entire book using Cineo Lighting gear. You can learn more about them at their website (www.cineolighting.com). For me, they are a dream come true: portable, cordless, color-correct, lightweight, with a comfortable operating temperature. Cineo Lights made these motorcycle shoots easier, faster, and safer. They gave me incredible consistency unlike anything I've used before.

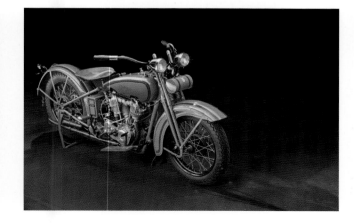

The technique is deceptively straightforward. First, of course, you need a spectacular car or motorcycle in front you in a room or outside location with no extraneous light. As for shooting, lock the camera in place on a tripod, focus it, and set the exposure (depending on the length of the vehicle) for somewhere between 8 and 15 seconds. Typically I use an aperture between f/11 and f/16—I adjust these exposures as I see the results. I turn on the light in my hand, turn out the room lights, open the camera shutter, and walk past the car at a steady speed with the light at a constant distance from the vehicle. The shutter closes. I do it again, back and forth across the vehicle, twenty or thirty times (more about this later). Motorcycle exposure times are shorter than cars, of course, because the vehicles are smaller. But also, the Cineo Lights offer much more light than even a 200-watt incandescent bulb in a soft box.

Whatever I do, I do *not* touch the camera during any of this activity—pixel-to-pixel registration is essential for image assembly.

Every time I see the image in my monitor, I'm amazed. A light streak will appear along the most beautiful character lines of the vehicle—its rooflines and rocker panels, or across motorcycle tanks, fenders, and engines. Why twenty or thirty passes? Make a pass with the light at ankle height, knee height, waist height, chest height, head height, and even overhead. Try letting the light rise and fall with the fender or roof contours. Then change from one Cineo Light—the Match Stix—to the Match Box. Then do it all over again.

With my previous lighting (soft boxes with incandescent light bulbs) I was constantly tripping over extension cords and stumbling into the cars or walls or other obstacles. The manageable Cineo lights allow me to easily and safely to maneuver around, along, and over the car or bike I'm shooting. The only thing I need to do is place a piece of tape over the power-on light. This will prevent an unwanted streak of light from appearing in my image. Cineo Lighting offers soft boxes for some of their lights as well as barn doors for their Match Stix. These lights offer just about the right amount of illumination and freedom needed to make this process work. Over time, I can imagine how the car or bike will look after each pass.

A friend introduced me to the CamRanger. This electronic device lets a photographer operate his modern-day auto-everything camera equipment by remote control. My friend fired his camera using his iPad mounted on a tripod, but he had to walk to see the image after each light pass. I prefer to use my iPhone because it saves time. I can modify aperture, shutter time, and even wirelessly adjust focus on auto-focus lenses. The benefit of this is I can light-paint without an assistant to "push the button." With my iPhone, I saw nearly instantly whether I'd succeeded or failed. I shoot RAW but the CamRanger works quickly with small jpegs so I reset my Nikon D810 to take both.

A friend likened his early experiences light-painting to learning to play three-dimensional chess wearing a blindfold. He could think about what he was doing but had no idea what it looked like, even when he could see his most recent exposure on the CamRanger screen. His advice was, "Shoot and keep shooting. Be sure you have enough passes." I'll add: when you believe you are done, start all over again and shoot more." This is not an obsessive-compulsive speaking but a recommendation borne from experience from one who did not follow important advice early and often.

I established a production goal of shooting two complete bikes in each ten- or eleven-hour day, five days a week. This meant a side profile view, a ¾ front, a ¾ rear, an engine view or two, and details. This proved ambitious, and I built up hundreds of files that were waiting for me to edit when I got home.

But did those exposures—or the dozen or more that I made—give me what I needed to define, describe, or sculpt the motorcycle or car? When I got to the computer and began stitching the views together was the moment of truth.

I've used Adobe Photoshop for years and made primary adjustments in color balance, contrast, shadow, and highlight preservation. As a light-painter, this was only the beginning. At this point in the process, it was all about the choices I made and those I was facing. Each light pass gave me a different feel or look. Remember, each pass is a different layer in Photoshop. Hopefully the end result—the book you are now holding—proves I made the right choices.

—Tom Loeser

Index